KV-039-482

NewPhilosopher

Editor
Zan Boag
Editorial Director
Antonia Case
Art Directors
Carlos Egan, Aida Novoa
Cover design
Genís Carreras
Editor-at-large
Nigel Warburton
Deputy Editor
André Dao
Contributors
Mariana Alessandri, Elizabeth Anderson, Matthew Beard, Marina Benjamin, Oliver Burkeman, Antonia Case, Tom Chatfield, André Dao, Tim Dean, Alexander Hinds, Tiffany Jenkins, Timothy Olds, Michael Puett, Clarissa Sebag-Montefiore, Patrick Stokes, Nigel Warburton
Illustrators / Artists
Genís Carreras, Carlos Egan, Yeiyei Gómez, Russel Herneman, Alvaro Hidalgo, Corey Mohler, Aida Novoa, Fabio Paolucci
Photographers
Charlotte Gilhooly, Hyo Lee, Charles K. Michael, Library of Congress, Wellcome Trust
Administration
Marnie Anderson, Claudio Faerman
Poet store
Jessica Davies, Prudence Hardcastle, Jack Suridge
Subscribe
newphilosopher.com/subscribe
Contact
130 Macquarie St Hobart Tasmania 7000 Australia
subscribe@newphilosopher.com
Distributors
AU/NZ: Gordon & Gotch;
UK/EU: Pineapple Media;
US/CAN: Disticor;
Digital: Apple iTunes, Google Play, Amazon Kindle, Zinio, EBSCO, Air France, KLM
Printers
Ovato (AU/NZ)
Wyndeham Bicester (UK/EU/US/CAN)

ISSN 2201-7151 Issue 24, #2/2019

#24

"Evermore in the world is this marvellous balance of beauty and disgust, magnificence and rats."

Ralph Waldo Emerson

Balance

On a balmy morning in August 1974, a young man walked on a steel cable between the Twin Towers in New York. For three-quarters of an hour Philippe Petit stunned onlookers as he performed this feat 400 metres off the ground, defying fear, gravity, and a stiff breeze.

"There is no why," Petit replied when asked about the motivation for his balancing act. But I suspect there was: to create order within disorder; harmony amongst discord. Life is, whether we like it or not, out of balance most of the time. We seek ways to rebalance and, once there, we try to maintain an equilibrium. Sleep more, work less. Laugh more, stress less. Listen more, talk less. Give more, take less. Risk more, fear less.

Nine years after his stunt, Petit's daughter Cordia Gypsy was born. Nine years later and she was gone, dead from a brain injury. "One has to find a balance between joy and sorrow," he remarked when asked about her death.

Petit walked on a wire in the sky and recovered from the death of his daughter, both times finding equilibrium in what seemed an impossible situation. We may not be funambulists, but we could do worse than to follow Petit's lead and seek balance when it appears there is none to be found.

Zan Boag

Zan Boag
Editor,
New Philosopher

Contents

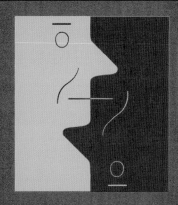

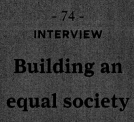

Balance

BUTOR CSARNOK
VARRÓGÉP RAKTÁR

Photo: Tightrope walker, Romania, Transylvania, Fortepan.

Online at

newphilosopher.com is an online portal for exploring philosophical ideas on ways to live a more fulfilling life. Read the articles, join in discussions, watch free online documentaries, and plan your trip to the next festival near you.

newphilosopher.com

newphilosopher.com/
articles/defining-ourselves/

What is it to be human?

Many of the problems in the world today, when one reflects upon them, call for an answer to an ancient question: What is it to be human?

newphilosopher.com/
articles/caught-in-the-web/

Caught in the web

In an age defined by increasing levels of hyper-connectivity, the question remains: is our technology truly bringing us closer together, or are we simply getting caught in the web?

newphilosopher.com/
articles/doing-away-
with-death/

The death of 'death'

With advances in medical science and technology comes the allure of defying death – and the 'life extension' movement is gaining momentum across the globe.

shop online

newphilosopher.com

NewPhilosopher

newphilosopher.com/shop

New Philosopher online store

Visit the online store for previous issues of *New Philosopher* magazine, subscriptions as well as gift ideas.

New Philosopher Writers' Award

Entries are open for the *New Philosopher* Prize for Philosophical Writing. Enter now to win $1,000 and have your work featured in the magazine.

Open to NP subscribers, award XXIV entries close 31 August 2019

Up to 1,500 words of fiction or non-fiction, based around the theme 'balance'. For more details and to enter online visit:

newphilosopher.com/prize

Subscribe now

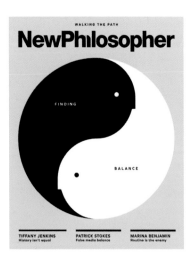

Delivered to your door

To receive your copy of the beautifully-designed, perfect-bound 132-page print version delivered directly to your door, subscribe now at:

www.newphilosopher.com/subscribe

NewPhilosopher
magazine

Purchase back issues and the current edition
online at newphilosopher.com.
The current edition is also available at newsstands,
bookstores, galleries, and airports worldwide.
Subscribe online at
newphilosopher.com/subscribe/

NewPhilosopher.com

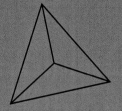
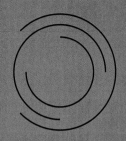

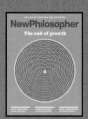

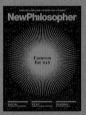

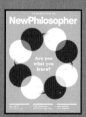

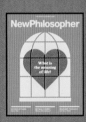

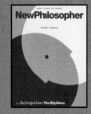

"New Philosopher is
one of the best things
happening."

"It utterly blew
me away."

"New Philosopher
has given me hope
for the future of
this country's media
landscape and for
the public discussion
emanating from it."

"I feel like I have
been waiting for this
magazine all my life."

"This magazine
is remarkable!"

"Fascinating and
challenging material,
attractively presented,
well bound – what
more could one ask?"

Contributors

Michael Puett

Michael Puett is the Walter C. Klein Professor of Chinese History and Anthropology, as well as the Chair of the Committee on the Study of Religion, at Harvard University. His interests are focused on the inter-relations between philosophy, anthropology, history, and religion, with the hope of bringing the study of China into larger historical and comparative frameworks. He is the author of *The Ambivalence of Creation*, *To Become a God*, and *The Path*.

Mariana Alessandri

Mariana Alessandri is Assistant Professor of Continental Philosophy, Existentialism, Philosophy of Religion, and Spanish-language Philosophy at the University of Texas-Rio Grande Valley. She has written for *The New York Times*, *Philosophy Today*, *Womankind* magazine, *Times Higher Education*, *Chronicle of Higher Education* and many academic journals. Her teaching interests include Existentialism and Mexican-American Philosophy.

Tim Dean

Tim Dean holds a doctorate in philosophy in evolution and morality from the University of New South Wales. Previously the Editor of *Cosmos*, Editor of *Australian Life Scientist*, and Science and Technology Editor at *The Conversation*, Dean is currently an Honorary Associate in the Philosophy Department at the University of Sydney. His work has appeared in *New Scientist*, *Popular Scientist*, *Cosmos*, *The Sydney Morning Herald*, and the *ABC*. In 2015 he was awarded the AAP Media Professionals' Award.

Elizabeth Anderson

Elizabeth Anderson is the Arthur F. Thurnau Professor and John Dewey Distinguished University Professor of Philosophy and Women's Studies. Her research includes equality in political philosophy, racial integration, and the ethical limits of markets. She is currently working on the history of egalitarianism, taking the history of abolitionism as a central case study. Anderson was the first Director of the Program in Philosophy, Politics, and Economics.

Patrick Stokes

Patrick Stokes is a lecturer in philosophy at Deakin University, Melbourne. He specialises in 19th and 20th century European philosophy, personal identity, narrative selfhood, moral psychology, and death and remembrance. A particular focus is bringing Kierkegaard into dialogue with contemporary analytic philosophy of personal identity and moral psychology. Stokes was awarded the 2014 AAP media prize.

Clarissa Sebag-Montefiore

Clarissa Sebag-Montefiore lived in China from 2009 to 2014, during which time she worked as the associate editor for *Time Out Beijing*, the art editor for *Time Out Shanghai*, and as an op-ed columnist for the *International New York Times*, reporting from China for the blog *Latitude: Views From Around the World*. She writes for *The Guardian*, *The Economist*, *Financial Times*, *The New York Times*, *Womankind*, *Wall Street Journal*, *New Statesman*, *New Internationalist*, *The Huffington Post*, and *Time* magazine.

Nigel Warburton

Nigel Warburton is a freelance philosopher, podcaster, writer, and the Editor-at-large of *New Philosopher*. Described as "one of the most-read popular philosophers of our time", his books include *A Little History of Philosophy*, *Thinking from A to Z*, and *Philosophy: The Classics*. The interviewer for the *Philosophy Bites* podcast, Warburton was previously Senior Lecturer in Philosophy at the Open University and Lecturer in Philosophy at Nottingham University.

Marina Benjamin

Marina Benjamin is the former arts editor of the *New Statesman* and deputy arts editor of the *Evening Standard*. A memoirist best known for *The Middlepause*, which offered a poetic and philosophical take on midlife, her new memoir *Insomnia* is forthcoming. Benjamin is a Senior Editor at *Aeon magazine*, a Consultant Fellow for the Royal Literary Fund, and a creative writing tutor at Arvon.

Oliver Burkeman

Oliver Burkeman is a writer based in New York. He is the winner of the Foreign Press Association's Young Journalist of the Year and was shortlisted for the Orwell Prize in 2006. His books include *HELP! How to Become Slightly Happier and Get a Bit More Done* and *The Antidote: Happiness for People Who Can't Stand Positive Thinking* – which explores the upsides of negativity, uncertainty, failure, and imperfection.

Zan Boag

Zan Boag is Editor of *New Philosopher*, Editorial Director of the international newsstand magazine *Womankind*, and director of *poet* bookstore. In 2017 he won the Australasian Association of Philosophy Media Professionals Award and was shortlisted for Editor of the Year in the international Stack Awards. Boag speaks regularly on philosophy, technology, the media, and ethics and is the co-founder and host of the monthly philosophical discussion series *Bright Thinking*. He is a Fellow of the Royal Society of the Arts.

Tiffany Jenkins

Tiffany Jenkins is an author, academic, and broadcaster. Her books include *Keeping Their Marbles* and *Contesting Human Remains in Museum Collections*, and she has written for *the Observer*, the *Financial Times*, *The Scotsman*, and *The Spectator*. She is an Honorary Fellow at the University of Edinburgh and a former visiting fellow at the London School of Economics. Jenkins holds a BA in art history and a PhD in sociology.

Matthew Beard

Matthew Beard is a moral philosopher with an academic background in applied and military ethics. He is an Associate Lecturer at the University of Notre Dame Australia and a Fellow at The Ethics Centre, undertaking research into ethical principles for technology. In 2016, he won the Australasian Association of Philosophy prize. He is a presenter on the ABC podcast Short & Curly, an award-winning children's podcast aimed at getting families to engage with ethics in a fun and accessible way.

Timothy Olds

Timothy Olds is Professor of Health Sciences at the University of South Australia. He holds two PhDs, one in French studies from the University of Sydney, another in exercise science. His research interests have been in mathematical modelling of cycling performance, anthropometry, and trends in fitness, fatness, physical activity and food intake. He was Project Director for the Australian National Nutrition and Physical Activity Survey.

Tom Chatfield

Tom Chatfield is a British writer, broadcaster, and tech philosopher. He is the author of six books, including Netymology, Live This Book!, and How to Thrive in the Digital Age, and speaks around the world on technology, the arts, and media. Chatfield was launch columnist for the BBC's worldwide technology site, BBC Future, is a Visiting Associate at the Oxford Internet Institute, and is a senior expert at the Global Governance Institute.

Genís Carreras

Genís Carreras is the designer of every cover of *New Philosopher* magazine and the creator of *Philographics: Big Ideas in Simple Shapes*. Carreras's work has been recognised in the AOI World Illustration Awards, the Laus Awards, and the Stocks Taylor Benson Awards, and his work has been featured in the books MIN: *New Simplicity in Graphic Design, Playing with Type, Geometry Makes Me Happy*, and *Geo/Graphics*.

Antonia Case

Antonia Case is Editorial Director of *New Philosopher*, Editor of *Womankind* magazine, and an award-winning writer and journalist. She was the winner of the 2013 Australasian Association of Philosophy Media Professionals' Award, and in 2016 and 2017 was shortlisted for Editor of the Year in the International Stack Awards. Case was selected as 'philosopher in residence' for the 2016 Brisbane Writers' Festival and is co-founder of the philosophical discussion series *Bright Thinking*.

André Dao

Deputy Editor of *New Philosopher*, André Dao is a writer of fiction and non-fiction. His work has appeared in *The Monthly*, *SBS True Stories*, *Meanjin*, and *Al Jazeera English*. He is the co-founder of *Behind the Wire*, an oral history project documenting people's experience of immigration detention in Australia. Formerly the editor-in-chief of *Right Now*, Dao was a finalist for the Australian Human Rights Commission's Young People's Medal in 2011.

Carlos Egan & Aida Novoa

Carlos Egan & Aida Novoa are the art directors of *New Philosopher* and *Womankind* magazine, as well as for *poet* tea, which is produced by the magazines' publishers. Their work for the publications has been recognised by AIGA, the oldest and largest organisation for design in the United States, as well as by *Computer Arts* magazine, *Desktop Mag*, and *Creative Journal*.

2015 European Artistic Gymnastics Championships, balance beam, Pauline Schaeffer.

Balancing your selves

"From the equality of rights springs identity of our highest interests; you cannot subvert your neighbour's rights without striking a dangerous blow at your own."

–Carl Schurz

Few political or social debates get very far now without someone invoking the spectre of 'identity politics'. More often than not, this language signals a clash between two competing views of what humans are. Are we self-directed individuals responsible for our own choices, or beings shaped and constrained by the labels and roles society and history give us?

The language may be new, but the problem is ancient and persistent. It was also a major flashpoint in 20th century French philosophy. Existentialists like Jean-Paul Sartre and Simone de Beauvoir insisted each of us is radically free and thus entirely responsible for our actions. Our backgrounds certainly matter to us, but can never determine us. The generation of French thinkers that followed thought the Existentialists naïve: our thoughts, words, and deeds, they claimed, are the products of linguistic, economic, and political forces beyond our ken.

The problem is far from abstract. In our everyday lives we tend to oscillate between these two ways of seeing ourselves and each other, often in self-serving and inconsistent ways. I'm a rugged individualist who plays by his own rules, you're a sheep who does what society expects of you; you could have acted differently if you'd really wanted to, I'm a victim of circumstance.

What the clash over 'identity politics' points to is the need to turn this tension at the heart of what each of us is into a productive balance. We are both answerable for our choices and enmeshed in and responsive to the networks of language, class, and culture that have formed us. We're not just the social roles we play, but we are those roles too; like it or not. Each of us is already a long way out on this tightrope. They say the trick to walking on a tightrope is to keep yourself very firmly centred – and that's harder than it sounds.

The world's 26 biggest hoarders

World out of balance

Last year, the world's richest 26 people owned as much wealth as the 3.8 billion people who make up the poorest half of humanity. The richest of those 26, Jeff Bezos – founder and CEO of Amazon – has a net worth somewhere north of $112 billion. According to Oxfam, just one per cent of that is equivalent to the health budget of Ethiopia. So, what does the world's richest man do with all that money?

Start a space tourism company, of course. Why? Because, says Bezos, he can't think of a better way to spend that much money: only space travel will be "expensive enough to be able to use that fortune".

At first glance, the world's second-richest person, Bill Gates, is spending his money very differently. The Bill and Melinda Gates Foundation's annual donations of around $4.7 billion is comparable to the aid budgets of entire countries like the Netherlands. But though the specifics of their spending might differ, the world's first 'centibillionaires' share the same structural problem. Gates, just like Bezos, has had a hard time finding worthy projects to spend all that money on. Gates's donations,

though generous, are still dwarfed by the overall size of his fortune. And even Bezos's space travel ambitions are *only* costing him $1 billion a year – not nearly enough to exhaust his billions by the end of his lifetime.

Which is the point, after all. As sociologist Georg Simmel said in the early 20th century during the 'Gilded Age' – the last great period of inexhaustible wealth and insupportable inequality – the power of the wealthy lies not in what they actually spend their money on, but the *potential* of what they could do with their fortunes. It's that potential that attracts media and politicians to billionaires like bears to honey. It's also why the billionaires, no matter how visionary or extravagant or philanthropic, will always tend towards hoarding rather than spending – to keep their bank balances as full of potential as possible.

"Never get so busy making a living that you forget to make a life."

-Dolly Parton

There's a popular piece of graffiti that says: "The Earth would be better off without us." It's easy to sympathise. Our species is guilty of throwing our planet's biosphere into disarray in only a few short centuries, and is likely to disrupt it even more in the coming millennia. Not only have we triggered the sixth mass extinction event in our planet's history, we may have precipitated our own demise by disrupting the very ecosystems that sustain us.

The graffiti artist's conception of 'better' was likely informed by the state of the world just prior to the emergence of human industry. This was a world of untrammelled forests, happy dodos, and 280 parts per million of carbon dioxide – a better world than one where bees are extinct, seas are swallowing cities, and whole continents are uninhabitable for human life.

If our actions do leave the world as a flooded greenhouse, the planet will eventually find a new equilibrium, just as it has done after every other mass extinction. New species will emerge and thrive in the hotter world. And in time, even they will die out only to be replaced by others.

But would this really be *better*? The only way we can judge whether any state of the world is 'better' or 'worse' is by comparing it to what suits us. But we can't do that if we're not around to judge. As philosopher and environmentalist Clive Hamilton puts it, "if humans were wiped from Earth the planet would not live on, not in any meaningful sense. For it is we who give the Earth meaning."

If that's the case, then perhaps it is not a matter of abdicating our responsibility and letting life find its own balance without us; instead, it's up to us to find a way that allows other species to thrive alongside us. Not just for nature's sake, but for ours.

Photo by Hyo Lee

The sensible centre

We tend to think that the correct answer to a problem must lie between two extremes. For instance, we often hear about the need to listen to "both sides of the argument", with the implicit assumption being that the truth – balanced somewhere between the two sides – will emerge from the adversarial process. But that assumption only works if the spectrum of belief is properly calibrated. It doesn't work, for instance, when the 'two sides' are belief in anthropogenic climate change and climate change denialism.

The same could be said for the two-party political system that dominates much of the English-speaking world. The accepted wisdom is that the two-party system encourages policymaking towards the 'sensible centre', as politicians vie for the majority of voters that fall between the 'Left' and 'Right' poles of the political compass. Yet the recent rise in populist politics in western democracies

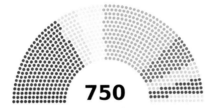

European parliament composition, 2017

hasn't bypassed two-party nations, which would be the expectation if the tendency towards centrism held true. Instead of balance, what we've seen is Left and Right parties – hollowed out by falling membership and fighting off minor parties – appealing not to the centre, but to their base.

Populism aside, the two-party system has also been criticised for failing to reflect the real diversity of views in the electorate. According to this criticism, the two parties do tend towards a 'centre', to the extent that Left/Right becomes indistinguishable, at least when it comes to significant public policy. The problem is that there's no reason to think that

this centre is 'sensible' – it could, for instance, just reflect elite consensus.

In contrast, multi-party systems – which are more prevalent in continental Europe – generally require more coalition-building between parties to form government. While that can lead to hung parliaments or political instability, it at least encourages us to think outside of the Left/Right binary – and to remember that balance isn't always found in the centre.

"In all sectors of society there should be roughly equal prospects of culture and achievement for everyone similarly motivated and endowed."

–John Rawls

Yin and Yang of the universe

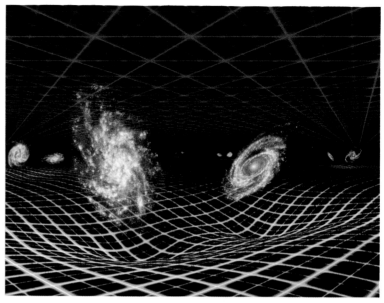

Source: NASA

Astronomers think that the expansion of the universe is regulated by both the force of gravity, which acts to slow it down, and a mysterious dark energy, which pushes matter and space apart. In fact, dark energy is thought to be pushing the cosmos apart at faster and faster speeds, causing our universe's expansion to accelerate.

In the artist's conception on this page, dark energy is represented by the purple grid above, and gravity by the green grid below. Gravity emanates from all matter in the universe, but its effects are localised and drop off quickly over large distances.

New results from NASA's Galaxy Evolution Explorer and the Anglo-Australian Telescope atop Siding Spring Mountain in Australia confirm that dark energy is a smooth, uniform force that now dominates over the effects of gravity.

The observations follow from careful measurements of the separations between pairs of galaxies (examples of such pairs are illustrated here). The results are one of the best confirmations of the nature of dark energy to date.

"No human face is exactly the same in its lines on each side, no leaf perfect in its lobes, no branch in its symmetry. All admit irregularity as they imply change; and to banish imperfection is to destroy expression, to check exertion, to paralyse vitality."
–John Ruskin

"Look, I'm busy. Do you have an ETA for inner peace?"

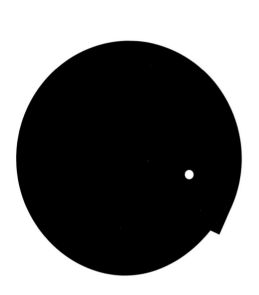

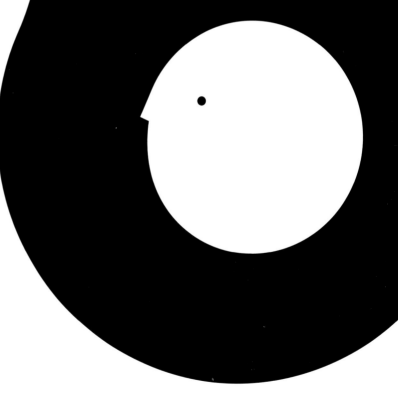

"There are
dark shadows
on the Earth ...

... but its lights
are stronger in
the contrast."

Charles Dickens

Illustration by Genís Carreras

BALANCE OF POWER

Australia (since 1901)

Liberal/National & predecessors **84** years — Labor **33.5** years

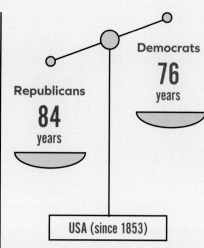

USA (since 1853)

Republicans **84** years — Democrats **76** years

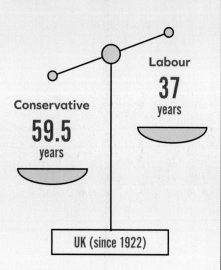

UK (since 1922)

Conservative **59.5** years — Labour **37** years

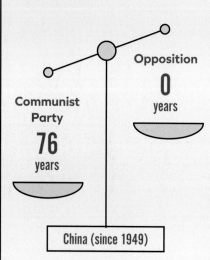

China (since 1949)

Communist Party **76** years — Opposition **0** years

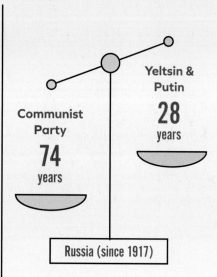

Russia (since 1917)

Communist Party **74** years — Yeltsin & Putin **28** years

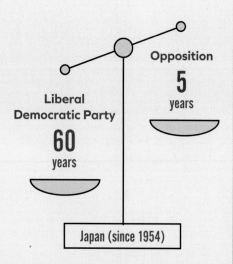

Japan (since 1954)

Liberal Democratic Party **60** years — Opposition **5** years

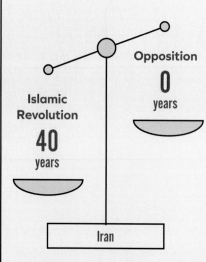

Iran

Islamic Revolution **40** years — Opposition **0** years

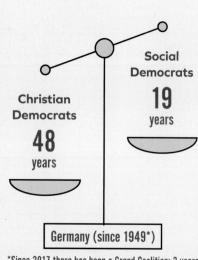

Germany (since 1949*)

Christian Democrats **48** years — Social Democrats **19** years

*Since 2017 there has been a Grand Coalition: 2 years

RIGHT OR OBLIGATION?

Voter turnout in the 2016 Australian Election (compulsory)

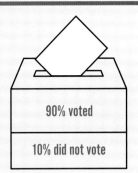

90% voted

10% did not vote

Total eligible voting population

Voter turnout in the 2016 US Presidential Election (non-compulsory)

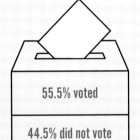

55.5% voted

44.5% did not vote

Total eligible voting population

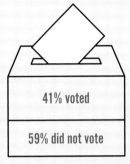

41% voted

59% did not vote

Earning less than $10,000 p.a.

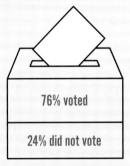

76% voted

24% did not vote

Earning more than $150,000 p.a.

Democratic vs authoritarian

According to *The Economist*'s 2018 Democracy Index, there are:

20
FULL DEMOCRACIES

(including Australia, Costa Rica, Mauritius, Uruguay, and the UK)

55
FLAWED DEMOCRACIES

(including the US, Japan, Israel, France, and Namibia)

39
HYBRID REGIMES

(including Fiji, Thailand, Nepal, Turkey, and Iraq)

53
AUTHORITARIAN REGIMES

(including China, Egypt, Russia, Iran, and North Korea)

75 FULL AND FLAWED DEMOCRACIES   versus   92 HYBRID AND AUTHORITARIAN REGIMES

47.7% of the world's population

52.3% of the world's population

Out of balance

by **Marina Benjamin**

In a madly spinning world, it is only natural that we should yearn to create points of stillness. We want the yin to balance the yang, the positive to counter all those negatives, and for push to meet pull. At the point of equilibrium (where there is no tension), we believe we will cease to be at war with ourselves, that we will find an inner peace. And yet, that elusive balance – when you do find it – is only ever temporary, or perhaps illusory, since everything is in constant flux anyway: life flows on, circumstances change, people themselves change and, with it, what they want changes as well.

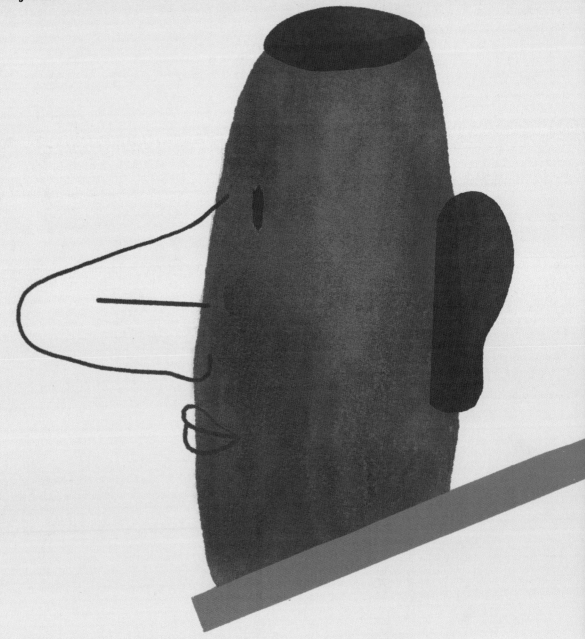

So it seems to me perverse that we're so quick to applaud the golden few who claim to have achieved a perfect balance, and who stare glowingly at us from the covers of lifestyle magazines, smug at having exquisitely calibrated every aspect of their lives into flawless harmony: their work life, home life, sex life, even their spiritual life. To look at the feature space these icons of wellness command – all glossy and manicured, from their children to their bank accounts – you'd think that they float through their days on clouds of contentment, smiling benignantly at everyone they meet, never feeling harried or burdened, never waking up in the night wracked with anxiety, never succumbing to distress, disappointment, depression or rage.

How did we get to the place where, by contrast, any expression of disproportionate hunger or desperate need, as well as any pronounced tendency towards excess, is viewed as a moral failing? The social opprobrium faced by alcoholics and drug addicts, for example, or by people who overeat or who perpetually chase after sex, is near universal, and can be readily gauged by the cultural pressure we place on such people to apologise for a failure to moderate. "I've got an addictive personality," they'll often say, with a sad shuffling of feet. Incapable of leading balanced lives, they are made to feel ashamed of their uncontrollable and lopsided hungers, guilty about wanting too much, too often. You cannot blame them for wishing to pass the

Illustration by Aida Novoa and Carlos Egan

buck by imputing their unruly cravings to an innate disposition – as if addiction were merely a matter of wiring, or even, if you're a 12-step aficionado, a disease.

Personally speaking, I'm happy to own up to my addictions. My drug of choice varies week by week, sometimes it is work, sometimes food; sometimes I'm just hungry for life experience. But the common aim in all these pursuits is to push beyond satiety, tramping over the idea that sensory experiences are best enjoyed in moderation, and embrace what it might mean to live *in extremis*. Who, after all, hasn't sometimes longed for a wash of *too muchness* through their daily life? Admittedly, it can feel overwhelming; but throwing over balance and pulling out all the censorious stops generates a reckless energy that can swerve you fruitfully off-piste. You might feel as if you're speeding down an untenably steep incline. But it is thrilling nonetheless. And you might discover something about yourself in the process.

My problem is that I am predisposed to idealise those who are famous for living out of balance: Emily Dickinson, with her passionate (and uncompromising) devotion to her art. Sylvia Plath, with her passionate devotion to Ted Hughes – so mad in love she bit his cheek. Vincent van Gogh and his fevered attempts to commit fleeting impressions of light and colour to canvas: when I look at van Gogh's crazed brushstrokes, what I see is a wild discontent. More artists and thinkers than I can list have

been slaves to their monomania. What drives them is the very opposite of a quest for balance and, I would contend, it is the source of their creativity. As Anaïs Nin wrote: "something is always born of excess: great art was born of great terrors, great loneliness, great inhibitions, instabilities".

Even those of us (the majority) not born to suffer for the sake of art must surely admit that too much balance in one's personal life is simply dull. I've always thought of routine as the enemy, and living in perfect balance is tantamount to making it your best friend. In mastering – read denying – your individual passions, but also shutting yourself off from experiencing any jolts to the system that arrive from the outside world, one can become out of touch, moribund.

Or, one begins to live through others. It is no accident that stable (that is balanced) households frequently give rise to teenagers who are perpetually out of whack. Thrown by hormones, teenagers are in any case prone to feel everything keenly; their diurnal

I've always thought of routine as the enemy, and living in perfect balance is tantamount to making it your best friend.

rhythms are out of sync with work-ing life; they rage and cry, then give themselves up to manic highs. Teen-agers are fundamentally off-key, radi-cally unstable. We tell ourselves they'll grow out of it and eventually calm down. But I suspect that a nostalgic tic in our adult make-up envies teenagers their wild abandon and attraction to extremes, not least the joy with which they experiment with everything, from new looks to new loves.

When I was a teenager my moth-er's regular mantra was "try everything, but in moderation". Her advice fell on deaf ears. Teenagers are at once tribal and individual, and both these aspects of their being call not for balance but for strongly-expressed leanings. You might be a Goth or a punk or mod, or whatever, but once you find your tribe you must profess your allegiance by ex-cluding everything else. Yet within the chosen tribe, teenagers are valued for their particularity. Boring, run-of-the-mill balance just doesn't cut it.

Of course, there is danger in being unbalanced (which is precisely why it is so thrilling). People can exhaust, even destroy, themselves through being slave to their passions or addictions. And ex-treme behaviour inevitably carries risks – and costs. Often, in fact, the price is paid by those around the person who is perennially out of kilter, since one person's freedom to be wild necessarily restricts the freedom of others. Perhaps it's a matter of balancing how much one is unbalanced? Could there be such a thing as strategic off-centeredness?

Then again, given that life on this planet is fast, messy, unpredictable, and out of control, perhaps we ought simply to embrace the chaos. Quest-ing after balance is like questing after every other impossible standard: hap-piness, perfection, contentment. We are bound to fall short. So drop it. Dive into the mess, surrender to the mad-ness. Most likely, it will all come good in the end, and at least you will have enjoyed the ride. ◼

"It's a fair point:
I did say 'round'. My bad."

Jury Selection

Existential Comics

Author/illustrator: Corey Mohler, Existential Comics. For more comics visit existentialcomics.com

Illustration by Yeyei Gómez

by Oliver Burkeman

Your shadow self

The experience will be familiar to anyone who's tried to change their lives by following the steps in a typical self-improvement manual: you get everything set up to implement your new habit – the sneakers waiting beside the door for your morning run, the carrot sticks you're going to chew instead of reaching for a cigarette – but then, when the moment arrives, you falter. A strange new mood has arrived, like an uninvited guest: it's not that you just can't be bothered to follow through on your plans, but that something inside you actively wants to sabotage them. Part of you wants to get fit, or quit smoking. But another part – a part of which you were unaware when you formulated the original goal – wants to assert its independence, to indulge its desires, to watch your virtuous plans go up in flames. And often enough, that's the part that triumphs.

The Swiss psychiatrist Carl Jung wouldn't have been surprised by your experience. You were previously unaware of that dark urge, he would argue, because it arose from your unconscious – that inner world of which, by definition, nobody can be aware. Specifically, it came from your "shadow", the hidden vault of personality traits that our conscious ego wants to reject because they clash with our ideal self-image, and which we consequently push out of awareness in an effort to keep them at bay. "The shadow personifies everything that the subject refuses to acknowledge about himself," Jung wrote. It's to the world of the shadow that we relegate all those things in ourselves that we learned, from early childhood, to see as unacceptable – along with various sexual and aggressive appetites we must repress if society is to function at all.

Jung's insights, like those of his immediate predecessor Sigmund Freud, have fared poorly in the face of the modern insistence on 'evidence-based' psychology. (That injury was partly self-inflicted, since both men insisted that their ideas should have the status of science; perhaps they should have

equated them instead with other paths to truth, such as philosophy or literature.) The very concept of the unconscious makes contemporary cognitive psychologists uneasy – if you're not even conscious of something, it's obviously rather hard to quantify it – and one recent book, *The Mind Is Flat* by the behavioural scientist Nick Chater, goes as far as to deny there's any such thing. Scientifically supported or not, however, the shadow remains an extremely useful tool for thinking about human behaviour – and how life goes wrong when we fail to find a balance between the parts of ourselves we're happy to admit to, and those we'd sooner deny.

It would be one thing if our attempts at repression actually worked. We might never come to know our murkier side, but at least life might run fairly smoothly. But Jung argued that we're rarely successful, for very long, in our efforts to deny the shadow. The more we repudiate it, attempting to live as if it didn't exist, "the blacker and denser it is", and the more powerful it gets – until it erupts into destructive external behaviour. As he famously declared: "That which we do not bring to consciousness appears in our lives as fate." If you imagine that you can give up (say) drinking merely by fiat – using your conscious ego to declare, "no more drinking from now on!", without examining the emotional wounds for which alcohol had been serving as the salve – then don't be surprised when your addiction fights back.

This also helps explain, for example, the now clichéd figure of the homophobic American church pastor who finds himself embroiled in a career-ending gay sex scandal. His homophobia represents his strenuous attempt to deny the truth about himself to himself, because he's learned to regard his sexuality as shameful. But while his public pronouncements may succeed in hurting others, they fail in their true goal of eradicating, or decisively taming, this aspect of his personality. Instead, that aspect only grows stronger, until it bursts forth in a life-disrupting way.

It's easy enough to see how this dynamic might explain the personality of a leader such as Donald Trump, who seems drawn with uncanny predictability into attacking his critics for precisely those flaws he seems unable to acknowledge in himself. But a more uncomfortable question is whether the shadow operates on a societal level, too – so that the very success of a politician like Trump represents the resurgence of something real that the culture has too long denied. One

criticism of liberal humanism is that it seeks to bring about a world free of violence and injustice merely by deciding it must be so – the political equivalent of deciding to be alcohol-free from this day on. But perhaps some darker aspects of human nature can't be so easily legislated out of existence. Perhaps some aggression or desire for superiority runs deeper in us – in which case it would make sense that these forces would erupt in alarming and extreme forms. Trump's campaign speeches painted a false picture of an America in violence and chaos. But they may have resonated, the writer Alexander Blum has speculated, partly because they acknowledged that violence and chaos are indeed part of who we are.

For Jung, there was no simple technique for dealing with the shadow. (The desire to 'deal with' unwelcome traits is, of course, just another way of denying their power.) All you can do, haltingly and imperfectly, is to find ways to bring it into consciousness, to acknowledge that it's there. "One does not become enlightened by imagining figures of light," he wrote, "but by making the darkness conscious." The shadow makes itself known by certain clues: moods, fantasies, impulses, and above all dreams. To stay receptive to such signs – to wonder what they might mean, rather than only seeking to change or ignore them – is to begin the journey of maturation Jung

called "individuation", starting from a willingness to entertain the possibility that there's more to your mind, and the collective mind of society, than you know.

It seems unlikely that neuroscientists will ever find evidence for the shadow's existence. But it retains so much value because of the stance of humility it represents. Self-help gurus, cognitive psychologists, and political commentators alike are prone to assuming that humans are psychologically transparent, at least to ourselves: that it's easy for us to understand our own personalities and motives, and thus similarly easy for us to alter ourselves, and our societies, like factory workers pulling levers on a machine. Jung reminds us not to be so sure – nor to assume, if we do shine a light in the darkness, that we'll necessarily like what we find.

The Jungian psychotherapist James Hollis once described the ego as a "thin wafer of consciousness, floating on an iridescent ocean called the soul". Plumbing that ocean can only ever be frightening, since if what's lurking there weren't at least somewhat scary, we'd never have consigned it to the depths in the first place. Still, there's comfort and camaraderie in the realisation that, when it comes to the intimidating vastness of what we don't yet know about ourselves, we are – to continue the nautical metaphor – all in the same boat. ◼

The shadow makes itself known by certain clues: moods, fantasies, impulses, and above all dreams.

In terms of wealth distribution, Credit Suisse reported in 2018 that the bottom half of the global population owns less than 1% of total wealth in the world. The top 1% owns 47% of all global assets.

At a global level, males slightly outnumber females 50.5%/49.5% (102 men for every 100 women). At birth, however, the 'natural' sex ratio is approximately 105 males to 100 females.

Some scientists, including Edward O. Wilson, have estimated that, in line with available water and food resources, a sustainable world population is likely to top out between 9 and 10 billion people.

The earliest Chinese characters for yin and yang date back to the 14th century BCE and are found in inscriptions made on 'oracle bones'.

In the OECD's work/life balance survey, the top 5 countries were Netherlands, Denmark, France, Spain, and Belgium. The bottom 5 were Turkey, Mexico, Israel, Korea, and Japan. Australia was the 9th worst (out of 38); USA the 10th worst.

Your sense of balance is called 'equilibrioception' and is generally based on a combination of senses including sight, vestibular balance (inner ear), and proprioception (your sense of the location of own body in space).

The World Economic Forum's Global Gender Gap Index Report reveals that pay disparity reduced by 0.03% in 2018 and has fallen 3.6% since the index started in 2006. At this rate, women will achieve parity in 202 years.

On the morning of August 7, 1974, then 24-year-old French high-wire artist and performer Philippe Petit illegally erected a wire between the Twin Towers of the World Trade Centre in New York City, performing 400 metres above the ground for 45 minutes.

The record for the fastest time to travel one mile (1.6 km) on foot while balancing a book on the head is 8 minutes 27 seconds and was set by Ashrita Furman (USA) at the Jamaica High School track in Queens, New York, on 29 July 2009.

In France, Italy, South Africa, and the UK, more than a third of seats in national parliament are held by women. In China, it is 25%. In the US, Pakistan, and Bangladesh the figure is 20%; in India it sits at just over 10%.

Famine to feast

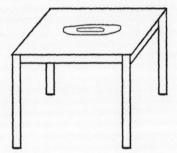

by Clarissa Sebag-Montefiore

The dogs had been stewed and the tree stripped of its bark. But it wasn't enough. In 1959, in the darkest depths of China's Great Famine, Yang Jisheng watched the uncle who raised him starve to death.

The experience led to journalist Yang's magnum opus: his book *Tombstone*, first published in 2008 in Hong Kong and translated into English in 2013. A direct outcome of Mao's catastrophic Great Leap Forward, Yang estimates that the 1959-61 famine left 36 million dead. Many resorted to eating corpses and violence was commonplace. In the name of Mao's larger goal of collectivised farming, the Communist Party stuck resolutely to its policies, with deadly consequences.

Yang, whom I met when I was a reporter in Beijing, told me he named his book *Tombstone* for one reason: to commemorate the dead – and in particular his uncle. This mattered in a country which to this day has largely erased the famine (euphemistically referred to by the Party as the "three years of natural disasters") from school history books and official tracts. *Tombstone* remains banned on the mainland, censorship is rife, and next to no physical memorials exist.

China has since gone from famine to feast. Following Deng Xiaoping's reforms, kick-started in 1978, it has transformed into an economic powerhouse. Today, food issues increasingly revolve around having too much, rather than too little: a glut of fast-food companies, combined with sedentary lifestyles and more office jobs, has led to a rise in obesity. A 2016 study in the medical journal *The Lancet* declared that China had overtaken the US as the country with the most obese people worldwide. It has led to what Paul French, co-author of *Fat China: How Expanding Waistlines are Changing a Nation*, once predicted to me – correctly – would be a "tsunami of lifestyle diseases".

Illustration by Aida Novoa & Carlos Egan

Food issues increasingly revolve around having too much, rather than too little.

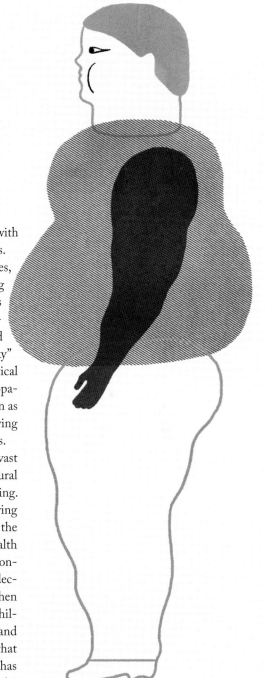

According to the study in *The Lancet*, 10.8 per cent of men and 14.9 per cent of women in China are now overweight – a total of 89 million people. With it has come a rise in type 2 diabetes and illnesses such as chronic kidney disease and cancer. There is also the issue of fat shaming: last year, in a viral video, an elderly passenger on the subway in Beijing tells off a younger, overweight man. "What is the matter with you? You are so fat!" the man says, adding: "Stay at home. Your overweight has affected others."

The incident caused outrage: many, both on social media sites and on the subway itself, rushed to the defence of the younger man. But if China as a nation now struggles with obesity, other issues around food have also crept in: namely, anorexia and bulimia.

Body image ideals, particularly for women, have transformed. For centuries, small features and tiny feet (created through the barbaric practice of foot binding) were lionised. Often, in ancient China, this was combined with a healthier reverence for plumpness.

One of the Four Great Beauties, Yang Yuhuan, a mistress of the Tang Dynasty's Emperor Xuanzong, was known for her larger physique. Under Chairman Mao, who believed that women held up "half the sky" and that their work ethic was critical to the success of communism, propaganda posters often showed women as ruddy-cheeked and robust, carrying grain on their (muscular) shoulders.

In China, until recently, the vast majority of the population was rural and survived off subsistence farming. A healthy sheen of fat (like having pale skin, unsullied by working in the fields) was considered a sign of wealth and abundance. It is a trend that continued to some degree into the decades of the one-child policy, when chubby 'little emperors' (or only children) were indulged by parents and grandparents who remembered what it was like to live without. Food has even entered everyday language: the

Seven plus-sized dancers performed, eager to show that fat could be statuesque.

greeting, "Have you eaten yet?" is akin in English to saying, "How are you?"

In many ways China, then, is no different to the west. Here, too, what is considered 'beautiful' when it comes to size has shifted over the decades. Dating to roughly 28,000 BCE, the *Venus of Willendorf*, a fertility statue discovered in 1908 in Austria, depicts a woman with her belly stretching over her groin and heavy, low-slung breasts. Michelangelo carved women in the Italian Renaissance with stomach rolls. Marilyn Monroe – Hollywood's most iconic sex symbol – was famously curvaceous.

Then there were the times when slim was considered best. The 1920s saw the growth of the 'flapper girl' who, ideally, was skinny and petite with small breasts and a lithe, boyish figure.

A similar ideal was sought after in the 1960s following British model Twiggy's rise to fame, feted for her twig-like limbs; and again in the 1990s, as Kate Moss's waifish heroin-chic look came to dominate magazine covers and catwalks.

Today, we have returned to a celebration of curves: reality TV stars have popularised the trend for big bottoms (and, more worryingly, for Brazilian butt lifts, the most dangerous cosmetic surgery procedure in the world). Corsets, too, with their emphasis on an hourglass figure, have come back into fashion as celebrities boast about 'waist training' (reducing the waist through corset-like garments). Designers such as Stella McCartney and Givenchy have also used the corset as key pieces in recent years.

And yet 'fat' is still seen as something to be ashamed of, that must be reduced through exercise, liposuction or dieting. My local hairdresser in Sydney is now offering fat-freezing sessions, alongside the cut and blow-drys. The message, propagated through social media and celebrity culture, is: you can be curvy as long as you are toned. You can have hips and a voluptuous butt, as long as you have a flat stomach and no double chin.

Some are reclaiming the word 'fat' as an identity to be proud of. In 2015, *Nothing to Lose* – a show put on by renowned Australian dance company Force Majeure – premiered in Sydney. Seven plus-sized dancers performed, eager to show that fat could be impressive, statuesque; beautiful even. As Kate Champion, director of *Nothing to Lose*, told me for an article I wrote for the BBC, "just putting a fat body on stage is a statement".

In the same article, Cat Pausè, a researcher in Fat Studies at Massey University, New Zealand, told me that "fat bodies are believed to be lazy, inactive, unattractive, asexual, unhealthy, unsuccessful, and unhappy". In the west, at least, fat for many equals not only ugly but somehow morally bankrupt.

So what does this for mean for China? There, too, the tide is turning as memories of the Great Famine fade; many young people remain unaware it happened at all. One social media trend saw women posting photographs of their waists to prove they were smaller than a 8.3 x 11.7 inch piece of paper. As Ning Yaxian, who has suffered from anorexia since the age of 14, told the *Los Angeles Times*: "People think if someone is skinny, it means that she is very successful." ◨

"When the Superior Person eats he does not try to stuff himself; at rest he does not seek perfect comfort; he is diligent in his work and careful in speech. He avails himself to people of the Tao and thereby corrects himself."

Confucius

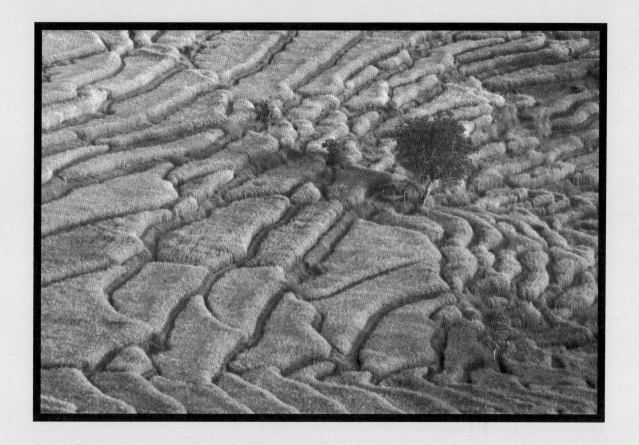

Photo: Kinari rice field, Indonesia, by Dion Bagindo

Balancing act

Illustration by Aida Novoa & Carlos Egan

Source: Guinness Book of Records

Most consecutive stairs climbed while balancing a person on the head
Who   Pablo Nonato Panduro, Joel Yaicate Saavedra
Where   Spain (Girona)
When   29 October 2018
Record 97 stairs

Greatest distance travelled on a bicycle balancing a football on the head
Who   Abdul Halim
Where   Bangladesh (Dhaka)
When   8 June 2017
Record 13.74 kilometres

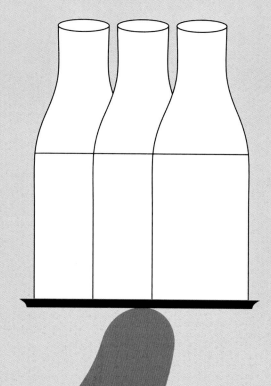

Most cups balanced on the forehead
Who   Konok Karmakar
Where   Bangladesh (Noakhali)
When   22 November 2018
Record 600 cups

Most eggs balanced by an individual
Who   Ashrita Furman
Where   USA (New York)
When   12 June 2010
Record 888 eggs

Most spoons balanced on the face
Who   Dalibor Jablanović
Where   Serbia
When   28 September 2013
Record 31 spoons

Tallest unicycle skipping
Who   Chaz Marquette
Where   USA (Venice Beach)
When   17 August 2003
Record 2.79 metres

Fastest time to swim 50 metres whilst balancing a football on the head
Who   Masud Rana
Where   Bangladesh (Dhaka)
When   2 August 2018
Record 44.95 seconds

Fastest 10m balancing cue on chin
Who   David Rush
Where   United States (Boise)
When   4 February 2017
Record 2.51 seconds

Fastest 100m with a can balanced on head (by a dog)
Who   Sweet Pea
Where   USA (Illinois)
When   3 September 2008
Record 2m55s

Longest duration balancing on a 6m ladder
Who   Uzeyer Novruzov
Where   China
When   7 January 2016
Record 7m15s

Most CDs balanced on one finger
Who   Silvio Sabba
Where   Italy (Milan)
When   12 July 2015
Record 247 CDs

Most open umbrellas balanced simultaneously
Who   Liu Lina
Where   Italy (Milan)
When   28 April 2011
Record 9 umbrellas

Most milk crates balanced on the head
Who   John Evans
Where   UK (London)
When   6 April 2001
Record 96 milk crates

Most beer kegs balanced on the head
Who   John Evans
Where   USA (Los Angeles)
When   17 June 1998
Record 11 beer kegs

Greatest distance cycled (no hands)
Who   V.T. Vignesh Kumar
Where   India (Madurai)
When   9 February 2017
Record 122 kilometres

Longest duration juggling five objects balanced on a ladder
Who   Emil Faltynek
Where   Tunisia (Kairouan)
When   23 March 2013
Record 56.92 seconds

Longest duration balancing on four fingers
Who   Wang Wei Bao
Where   China (Beijing)
When   9 November 2008
Record 19.23 seconds

Longest time treading water whilst balancing a football on the head
Who   Jhoen Lefont Rodríguez
Where   Cuba (Havana)
When   22 February 2018
Record 15m12s

Longest no-hands motorcycle wheelie
Who   AC Farias
Where   Netherlands (Amsterdam)
When   22 October 2004
Record 89 metres

Fastest mile balancing a football on the head
Who   Yee Ming Low
Where   Malaysia (Kuala Lumpur)
When   20 March 2010
Record 8m35s

False balance?

by Patrick Stokes

In March 2018, a man named Mike Hughes climbed into a home-made, steam-powered rocket, and launched himself 700 metres above the Mojave Desert floor. Thankfully, he came back down in one piece, if a little sore.

Like most of us, Mike is entranced by the idea of going into space. Unlike most of us, he wants to do so (at horrendous risk to his life) because he believes the world is flat, and wants to see for himself. "Do I believe the Earth is shaped like a frisbee? I believe it is. Do I know for sure? No. That's why I want to go up in space."

Modern flat-earthers have been around for more than two centuries, but in the internet age two interesting shifts seem to have occurred. Firstly,

Flat Earth belief has become more prominent, if still decidedly fringe. Becoming a flat-earther is the ultimate act of epistemic rebellion: what better way to declare yourself a free-thinking individualist than to deny a fact everyone else agrees on?

Secondly, the term 'flat-earther' itself has become a sort of shorthand for someone who believes something so outrageous that *nobody* is obliged to take their views seriously. A 'flat-earther' is not simply someone who believes something ridiculous; they're someone whose views are so far beyond the pale we don't need to listen to them at all.

Perhaps that's why we never see flat-earthers interviewed on TV shows about space travel or geography for the sake of 'balance'. I'm guessing flat-earthers themselves find this fact deeply unjust, if not downright sinister. (No doubt someone is writing a letter to *New Philosopher* right now to ask why we're taking part in the Round Earth conspiracy). But the rest of us aren't troubled by this exclusion.

On plenty of other topics, however, we get very uncomfortable indeed if the

media doesn't seek out comment from a range of voices. We want our news and our current affairs commentary to canvass all the relevant views instead of pushing a particular line. We want the media to be 'balanced'. This seems to be true even of people who seek out media with a particular ideological bent: even Fox News used to sell itself with the slogan *Fair and Balanced*.

As a journalistic virtue, the benefit of balance is obvious. We look to the media not simply to tell us how things are, but to represent uncertainty fairly too. If all questions of fact and value had clear and unambiguous answers, the media would simply be a conduit for information. But that's not the world we live in. Our epistemic limitations and the reality of moral and political disagreement means the media also has a role to play as a venue for controversies to play out. If there's disagreement, we want to hear all sides of that disagreement so we can make up our own minds.

That demand is linked to a major shift that's generally reckoned to have happened in the 18th century. We learned, so the story goes, to think for

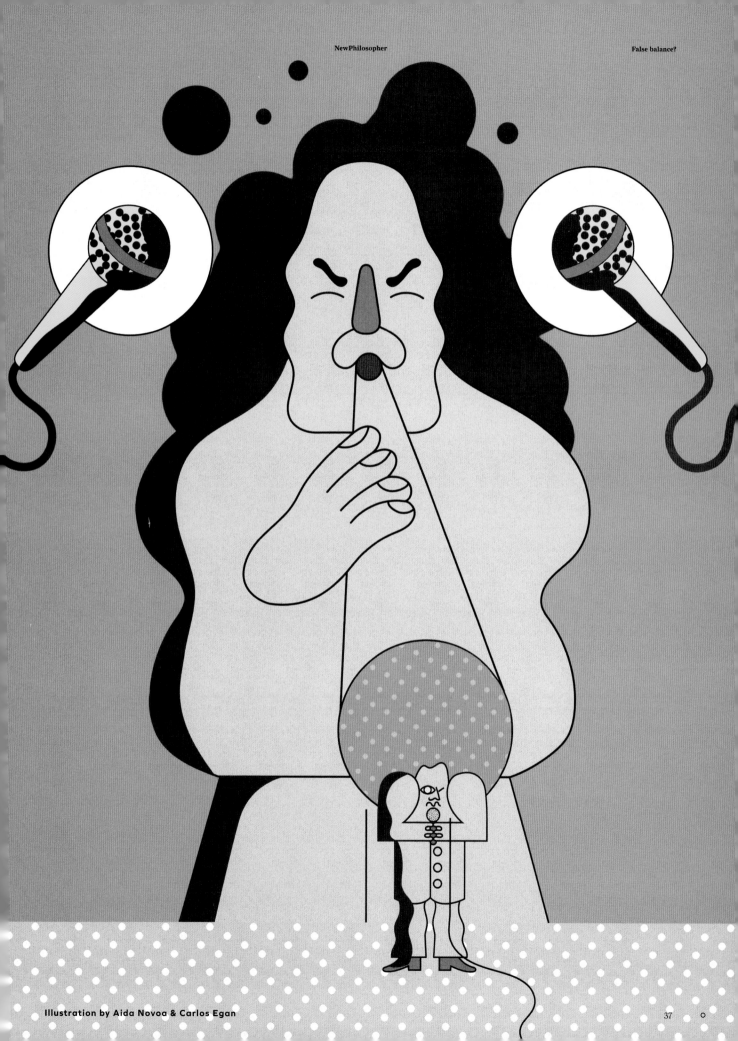

Illustration by Aida Novoa & Carlos Egan

ourselves. *Sapere aude*, declared Immanuel Kant: "dare to know", that is, to work things out for yourself, not simply to accept whatever the King or the Church tells you. Kant's attitude finds expression in such unlikely places as Fox News's updated slogan: *We Report. You Decide.*

Balance is, at heart, a sort of fairness, both to the participants in a controversy and to the viewer. It's a virtue journalists take on board very early in their training. In the main, journalists want to present themselves as objective, neutral brokers rather than partisans for a particular position. (Fox was widely condemned for not living up to *Fair and Balanced*, but not for the ideal itself).

But balance-as-neutrality has serious limits. To see why, ask yourself *why* we don't have flat-earthers on TV to provide 'balance' in stories about space travel. The answer might seem obvious: if flat earth belief is ridiculous (and it is), then we don't need to treat it as if it might be true.

Balance always operates against a background of decisions, implicit or overt, about whose voices need to be considered and which claims are serious ones. Life is short and news programs are even shorter, and that means we need to cut a few corners. "Had we but world enough, and time", to borrow a phrase from the 17th century poet Andrew Marvell, we could consider every viewpoint, every argument, even the very silly or very obnoxious ones. But we don't have that luxury. There's a notorious conspiracy theory, associated with the writer David Icke, that the British royal family are shape-shifting interdimensional reptilians. Yet it seems clear we don't have to work a *What if she's a lizard?* angle into every news item about the Queen.

So perhaps, surprisingly, 'balance' comes into play in a context of largely-settled consensus about *which* views don't warrant airtime. It's simply not possible to include every voice. Some views might also be left out because they are so hateful or harmful that we judge they have no place in civil discourse. In other cases, it would be outrageous *not* to give certain people the chance to speak, for instance where someone deserves a right of reply about allegations against them. But in between these extremes there's an enormous amount left to the individual judgement of producers and presenters.

The problem is that very often the controversy in question is over whether there even *is* a controversy to begin with. Some people think the world is flat: does that mean the shape of the world is a controversial topic? If you think the mere fact of disagreement means there's a controversy there, then pretty much any topic you care to mention will turn out to be controversial if you look hard enough. But in a more substantial sense, there's no real controversy here at all. The scientific journals aren't full of heated arguments over the shape of the planet. The university geography departments aren't divided into warring camps of flattists and spherists. There is no serious flat-earth research program in the geology literature.

So far, so obvious. But think about certain other scientific 'controversies' where competing arguments

We look to the media not simply to tell us how things are, but to represent uncertainty fairly too.

do get media time, such as climate change, or the safety and efficacy of vaccination. On the one side you have the overwhelming weight of expert opinion; on the other side amateur, bad-faith pseudoscience. In the substantial sense there aren't even 'two sides' here after all.

Yet that's not what we see; we just see two talking heads, offering competing views. The very fact both 'heads' were invited to speak suggests someone, somewhere has decided they are worth listening to. In other words, the very format implicitly drags every viewpoint to the same level and treats them as serious candidates for being true. That's fine, you might reply: *sapere aude*! Smart and savvy viewers will see the bad arguments or shoddy claims for what they are, right? Except there's some evidence that precisely the opposite happens. The message that actually sticks with viewers is not "the bad or pseudoscientific arguments are nonsense", but rather that "there's a real controversy here".

There's a name for this levelling phenomenon: *false balance.* The naïve view of balance versus bias contains no room for 'true' versus 'false' balance. Introducing a truth-value means we are not simply talking about neutrality anymore – which, as we've seen, nobody can or should achieve *fully* anyway. False balance occurs when we let in views that haven't earned their place, or treat non-credible views as deserving the same seat at the table.

To avoid false balance, the media needs to make important and context-sensitive discriminations about what is a credible voice and what isn't. They need balance as a verb, rather than a noun. To balance is an act, one that requires ongoing effort and constant readjustment. The risk, after all, is falling – perhaps right off the edge of the world. ◘

"My newspaper is perfectly balanced: gossip at the front, hearsay at the back."

Illustration by Fabio Paolucci

by **Mariana Alessandri**

There are no Mothers

Janelle Hanchett recently published a memoir about raising multiple children as a non-functioning alcoholic and drug addict. *I'm Just Happy to Be Here* shows the author heaving her recalcitrant body into the straitjacket of ordinary life. For years she couldn't do it. Her kids got taken away, multiple times and for multi-year stretches, while a sodden Hanchett raged against mediocrity. Like so many mothers today, she felt destined to more than a domestic life. Except for the 72-hour benders, gross negligence, and domestic violence, her story is relatable. Mothers everywhere want to be more

than just mothers. I suggest that we stop being them altogether.

Hanchett's life was far from balanced. She threw herself into serial identities as though each had the power to define her once and for all: Student, Mother, Wife, Addict. For Jean-Paul Sartre, adopting fixed identities is an attempt to dodge our freedom, the transcendent part of us that stubbornly exceeds our grounded, imminent selves. For Sartre, freedom is more burden than blessing, and he says that we try to skirt it more often than we realise. Instead of bearing freedom's weight, for example, many of us hitch ourselves to convenient jobs, spouses, or lives that we later come to resent. Sartre believed it is easier to contort ourselves to fit society's pre-prescribed roles than to admit that we don't have to. It's as though we make decisions behind our own backs,

and then wonder how we ended up here, in a life we didn't choose. Some of us are so wary of freedom that we are willing to adopt the label 'screw-up' rather than admit that we're making one bad choice after another. The most desperate among us – and perhaps the most existentially astute, like Hanchett – will do anything to deny our freedom, including tricking ourselves into believing that we're acting freely. If Hanchett had been an existentialist, she might have concluded that it's easier to be chained to alcohol than freedom. When you're free, you're responsible for where you end up. And if your worst fear, like hers was, is failing to live up to your potential, then why not throw the game? At least you could say that you never stood a chance. Sartre believed that we cheat ourselves daily, in serious and trivial ways alike.

Illustration by Aida Novoa & Carlos Egan

Like Hanchett, many of us long for an undeniable, inescapable challenge – a chance to become somebody, something. A mother, perhaps. But such desire is based on the misunderstanding that Mothers exist. It's to make Mother a noun. On Sartre's reading, there are no Mothers. Or Screw-Ups. Or Waiters, or Accountants, or Philosophers. These are just roles that we play. In trying to cast off our subjectivity we succumb to what Sartre calls "bad faith". Affairs are perhaps the easiest cases of bad faith to diagnose. A cheater announces that she's no longer in control of herself, that she's not responsible for her actions. *I can't help it* is bad faith's motto. Busyness is its accomplice. Keeping busy is the way we moderns avoid the existential crisis that would surely come from an honest look in the mirror. But we can't avoid the mirror forever, and Sartre said we can never fully lie to ourselves either, thanks to our transcendence. Hanchett thinks like an existentialist when she writes that at some point, alcohol stopped working. Freedom had outrun her, at which point she began recognising junkies as junkies. After years of playing the Screw-Up-Terrible-Parent-Drug-Addict, Hanchett admitted that she was free.

Like the alcoholic, the workaholic exercises her right to reject parenthood's mundane responsibilities, like bathing and feeding toddlers, but she does so dishonestly. She pretends she has no choice because of whatever noun she's trying to become. Perhaps Very Busy Mother, or Successful Career Woman. The first step in combatting bad faith is recognising that these characters don't exist. They are just roles that we play, none of which cancels out our transcendence. Admitting that we play multiple roles can give us

some of the grounding that Sartre says we crave minus the collateral damage of our imagined consequence-free behaviour. It can also keep us from seeking an identity to shield us from freedom. The Sartrean corrective to bad faith? Quit being a Mother.

I don't have to be a workaholic to know that office work gets me out of

Owning our feelings and especially our actions constitutes a rejection of bad faith.

taking care of my kids, so if I don't feel like doing it, I should just admit it. When I was still a Mother, I invented reasons not to play with my kids, but I felt too guilty to own up to it. After all, Mothers want to play with their kids. Cooking had always been a common way for me to buy myself time, but as a Mother in bad faith, I acted as though I were making a sacrifice for my family. Then Sartre stepped in to translate for me. He said that when I said I was busy cooking in the kitchen, what I meant was, see me as more than for-you. I'm also for-others. I'm for-my-friends and for-my-spouse and, sometimes, most importantly, for-myself. Sartre got me to admit that I get tired, that I crave time to think, that I like to be alone. Owning our feelings and especially our actions constitutes a rejection of bad faith. And rejecting Mothers helps too.

Since I've stopped being a Mother I no longer live for my children (which in many US contexts is almost heretical to admit). I live alongside them and I take care of them. Daily, they watch me play at being a mother, woman, teacher, cook, activist, friend,

writer, daughter, sister, etc. These roles are not in direct competition, though they do sometimes conflict. Recently, when I told my six-year-old I would be going on a short beach vacation with my best friend, he asked: "Why do you want to leave me?" I answered honestly: "I don't want to leave you, but I do want to join my friend at the beach." Over the years I have learned that playing a teacher makes me better at playing a mother, playing a mother makes me better at playing a daughter, and that playing a friend certainly makes me better at playing everything else. As long as we are choosing non-abusive and non-deceptive means, it's good for children to see that we play roles but aren't reducible to any one of them.

Life is existential play, thought Sartre. But there is no balance to be found in his theory. The work/life balance metaphor pretends that work and life are the only two factors that count toward a successful existence, and that these two poles must always be held in check, perfectly balanced. This faulty narrative ignores that we are complex and variable, always existing and always playing. It also assumes that balance is better than imbalance, which I doubt. Worst of all, it paints Mothers as objects and not players. Sartre would say that instead of trying to achieve work/life balance, we should get busy playing our existential roles, freely and responsibly. This begins when we quit being Mothers. ▢

"The sorrowful dislike the gay, and the gay the sorrowful."

Horace

Weighing of the heart

Artwork: Relief in the interior of the Hathor Temple of Deir el-Medina, in West Thebes at Luxor, Egypt

The Book of the Dead is an ancient Egyptian funerary text. The section pictured here shows the 'Judgement of the Dead': in a ceremony called 'the weighing of the heart', the deceased's ethical actions are weighed by Anubis against the feather of Maat, the goddess of truth, balance, order, harmony, law, morality, and justice. If the heart was found to be lighter or equal in weight to the feather of Maat, it was determined that the deceased had led a virtuous life and would go on to Aaru (heavenly paradise). One version of *The Book of the Dead* was acquired by Caspar Reuvens, the founding director of the Rijksmuseum van Oudheden (the Dutch National Museum of Antiquities). It was his final acquisition: on the trip back to the Netherlands he died from a stroke, with *The Book of the Dead* packed in his luggage.

Opposites are complementary

by Tim Dean

Illustration by Aida Novoa & Carlos Egan

In 1947, the Danish quantum physicist Niels Bohr faced a dilemma. The newly-minted King of Denmark, Frederick IX, had just surprised Bohr by announcing that he was to be awarded the Order of the Elephant, Denmark's highest order of chivalry, in recognition of his contributions to science. This was a remarkable achievement, not least because the Order of the Elephant was normally reserved only for royalty and heads of state, and Bohr was a mere commoner. In fact, only one other scientist had ever been awarded the Order of the Elephant in its 500-year history, and that was the Danish astronomer Tycho Brahe (who had the advantage of already being nobility).

In addition to receiving a rather hefty gold collar supporting an elephant-shaped badge, the recipient was also entitled to have their coat of arms displayed at Frederiksborg Castle,

north of Copenhagen. The problem was that Bohr, not being of noble birth, didn't actually have a coat of arms. So he decided to design his own.

At first, he looked to the Danish heraldic authority, the Statens Heraldiske Konsulent, for inspiration but found nothing that was to his liking. Then the dragon that he requested was turned down on the basis that it was not among the accepted Danish heraldic animals. This left him in a quandary as to what to choose.

The solution finally emerged from a conversation with a close friend, Hanna Kobylinski Rozental, an accomplished philosopher who had worked with the German phenomenologist Edmund Husserl. Rozental knew Bohr's work well, particularly his interest in the seemingly impossible task of reconciling the opposing worlds of quantum mechanics and classical physics. She also happened to be an expert in Chinese history and philosophy, so she suggested Bohr consider the symbol *taijitu*, better known as yin-yang. Bohr was thrilled with the idea and, to his joy, it was accepted for his coat of arms.

Bohr also had to choose a motto. This was an easier task. He quickly

settled on *contraria sunt complementa*, meaning "opposites are complementary". This is an abbreviated version of one of his favourite phrases: *contraria non contradictoria sed complementa sunt*, meaning "opposites are not contradictory, they're complementary".

Bohr's new coat of arms, resplendent with the yin-yang symbol and his paradoxical motto, reflected what he considered to be a deep truth about reality. It was a truth long acknowledged in eastern philosophy, and one he believed was underappreciated by many of his western scientific peers. It was the idea that there is no single schema, no single explanation, no single system of logic or thinking that is able to explain all of reality on its own. Rather, it takes multiple perspectives, often conflicting or contradictory, in order to make full sense of reality. It was an idea that Bohr referred to as the principle of complementarity, and he spent much of his career attempting to convince the western scientific community of its importance, often falling on deaf ears.

The principle was very much a product of Bohr's experience working at the forefront of quantum mechanics in the

It takes multiple perspectives, often conflicting or contradictory, in order to make full sense of reality.

first two decades of the 20th century. This was a tumultuous period, during which our understanding of the universe at its most fundamental level was being radically challenged. For centuries, it was the classical view of reality that dominated scientific thinking. This was the picture so elegantly outlined by Isaac Newton in the *Principia Mathematica* in 1687. It was the triumphant realm of elliptical planetary orbits, roaring steam engines, and the Scientific Revolution. The discovery of atoms in the 19th century only underscored the idea that the universe is nothing more than a cosmic billiard table, with atomic balls bouncing around following fixed causal laws.

It was a soothing picture. It reinforced the idea of a concrete objective reality 'out there', of which we are mere subjective observers. It also wrapped the universe in a neat deterministic ribbon, so if you happened to be the hypothetical omniscient demon described by Pierre-Simon Laplace in 1814, and you knew where all the balls started off and all the forces exerted

upon them, then you'd know with absolute certainty where they will be until the end of time. Even the weirdness of Albert Einstein's special and general theories of relativity only curved the billiard table, but they left the nice clean deterministic picture of classical reality intact.

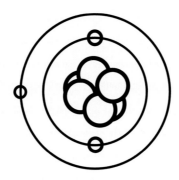

Then, at the very turn of the 20th century, quantum mechanics entered the room and upended the table. The quantum picture of the world that emerged over the following two decades, to which Bohr contributed a great deal, was utterly different to that offered by the classical view. At

the quantum level, it seemed like we were playing an entirely different game. The balls weren't just balls; they were also waves. They could be in two places at the same time. They did not even occupy any particular point but were instead a statistical smear across space and time. It even eroded the very distinction between the table and the player.

The quantum picture of the world was a lot less soothing than the classical one. It so subverted our intuitive understanding of how the world must be that many scientists came to the conclusion that it must be false. One of the doubters was Albert Einstein, who had even helped lay some of the foundations of quantum physics himself. Einstein engaged in a multi-decade debate with Bohr over the fundamental nature of reality, famously arguing that he couldn't accept that reality was governed by probabilities rather than certainties. Bohr, reflecting on this debate, wrote in 1949 that "Einstein mockingly asked us whether we could really believe that

The discovery of atoms in the 19th century only underscored the idea that the universe is nothing more than a cosmic billiard table.

the providential authorities took recourse to dice-playing" – i.e. God does not play dice.

For Bohr, 'God' really did play dice, at least at the quantum level. But this didn't diminish the truth of what we observe at the classical level. This is at the heart of the principle of complementarity. He argued that we have two different descriptions of reality – the quantum and the classical – and they disagree about fundamental things. But Bohr saw no contradiction. Both were equally true, and both were required to fully understand reality. The descriptions were not in opposition; rather they were complementary.

It's fitting that Bohr turned to eastern iconography in order to represent his views on complementarity. In many branches of eastern philosophy, the idea that there could be a singular precise description of reality, one that is objective and devoid of contradiction, is absurd. Rather, a by-product of using concepts to describe reality is that we also create opposites and contradictions. We become the architects of our own paradoxes. This isn't an indication that we have gotten something horribly wrong; it's just the way things are.

This is a dominant theme in the *Daodejing*, written by Laozi around the 6th century BCE, which itself is riddled with contradictions and paradoxes. This is reflected in the opening lines, often translated as: "The Dao that can be spoken is not the enduring Dao; The name that can be named is not the enduring name." There's no small amount of irony that the *Daodejing* deliberately uses words to show that truth is beyond words.

It's a sentiment that Bohr whole-heartedly agreed with. Another of his favourite sayings was that there were two kinds of truths. The first were "trivial truths", which were so obviously true that their negation was clearly false. Then there were "deep truths", which could be distinguished from the trivial variety because their negation was another deep truth.

Bohr never did manage to change Einstein's mind. But his principle of complementarity was more readily accepted by many scientists in Asia. Léon Rosenfeld – a close collaborator of Bohr's – discovered this when he travelled to Japan in 1961 to meet with Hideki Yukawa, who had done pioneering work on subatomic particles. Rosenfeld asked Yukawa whether Japanese physicists had struggled to accept Bohr's principle of complementarity. Rosenfeld wrote that "[Yukawa] answered, 'No, Bohr's argumentation has always appeared quite evident to us'; and, as I expressed surprise, he added, with his aristocratic smile, 'You see, we in Japan have not been corrupted by Aristotle.'"

"Prosperity is no just scale; adversity is the only balance to weigh friends."

Plutarch

"In its majestic equality, the law forbids rich and poor alike to sleep under bridges, beg in the streets, and steal loaves of bread."

Anatole France

"Men achieve tranquillity through moderation in pleasure and through the symmetry of life."

Democritus

"Something is always born of excess: great art was born of great terror, great loneliness, great inhibitions, instabilities, and it always balances them."

Anaïs Nin

"The fault of the utilitarian doctrine is that it mistakes impersonality for impartiality."

John Rawls

"Don't confuse symmetry with balance."

Tom Robbins

"The proper amount of wealth is that which neither descends to poverty nor is far distant from it."

Seneca

"In judging of others a man laboreth in vain… How seldom we weigh our neighbour in the same balance with ourselves."

Thomas à Kempis

"Toleration is the greatest gift of the mind; it requires the same effort of the brain that it takes to balance oneself on a bicycle."

Hellen Keller

Balance

"Your deepest presence is in every small contracting and expanding, the two as beautifully balanced and coordinated as birds' wings."

Rumi

"There is no hour that has not its births of gladness and despair."

George Eliot

"By the mean of the thing I denote a point equally distant from either extreme, which is one and the same for everybody."

Aristotle

"To be perfectly symmetrical is to be perfectly dead."

Igor Stravinsky

"It is not until a community or an individual has advanced a fair distance along the path of civilisation… that it can bear to admit the equality of women."

Rebecca West

"Is it so strange that losses balance gains?"

The Tale of Kieu

"Almost every wise saying has an opposite one, no less wise, to balance it."
George Santayana

"How one walks through the world, the endless small adjustments of balance, is affected by the shifting weights of beautiful things."
Elaine Scarry

"Any order is a balancing act of extreme precariousness."
Walter Benjamin

Illustration by Aida Novoa & Carlos Egan

Illustration by Aida Novoa & Carlos Egan

by **Tom Chatfield**

A balanced life

Is balance a self-evident good? It certainly thinks it is. Take a cliché like 'work-life balance'. To be out of balance is by definition to get something wrong. Perhaps you're working too hard, or not enough, or exhibiting insufficient *joie de vivre*. In any of these cases, what you need to do is obvious (even if doing it is difficult). You must weigh up your options and commitments, then find a way to bring yourself back into balance.

Philosophically speaking, the principle of balanced living owes a lot to Aristotle. In the *Nicomachean Ethics*, Aristotle uses the metaphor of a craftsman creating an excellent work to illustrate his ideal of the golden mean. Excellence in art or craft, he argues, describes a point where nothing remains either to be added or taken away – because to do either would diminish the

result. The achievement is an equipoise that's the opposite of average.

Aristotle has plenty of complex things to say about balance, purpose, and virtue – but few of these have made it as far as Silicon Valley, where technology facilitates one of the most influential modern implementations of balance as a philosophy of living. Assisted by ever-more assiduous systems, a happily productive 21st century citizen is one who quantifies and balances their diet, exercise, consumption, and career. Perfection is a precision-engineered existence whose outputs are monitored across all fronts: income, pleasure, leisure, lifespan. What's not to like about harmonising your life using the best tools available?

One objection to this vision of human thriving is suggested by the engineering metaphor itself. Every technology requires a set of assumptions about inputs and outputs: what goes into a system, what ought to come out, and what processes can best ensure this. In this sense, every machine is also a philosophy – the automated embodiment of a set of values. And these values entail fundamental judgements about what does, and doesn't, count.

Writing in *Harper's* magazine under the headline "Home of the Whopper", the essayist Thomas Frank envisions the chain-food restaurants that girdle America's cities in these terms: as technologies of inhumanly impeccable poise, balancing countless components in the service of productive harmony. "The modular construction, the application of assembly-line techniques to food service, the twin-basket fryers and bulk condiment dispensers, even the clever plastic lids on the coffee cups, with their fold-back sip tabs: these were all triumphs of human ingenuity," Frank notes. And yet: "that intense, concentrated efficiency also demanded a fantastic wastefulness elsewhere – of fuel, of air-conditioning, of land, of landfill. Inside the box was a masterpiece of industrial engineering; outside the box were things and people that existed merely to be used up."

Inside the box, like a mechanised master craftsman, the system moves in pursuit of a certain perfection – neither too much nor too little of any element; every bottleneck, delay or scrap of waste addressed and improved over time. Outside the box, however, there is only unquantified waste: materials inessential to the balancing act and thus weightless in its terms.

Balance seems a self-evident good precisely because it presupposes the rightness of the system it exists within: the virtue of a chosen mean, the value of a chosen task. And the more immaculately engineered the systems we act within, the more their incentives and values can come to seem synonymous with our own – and with those any right-thinking citizen should desire.

Aristotle had strict views about the ends it was, and was not, virtuous to pursue (self-improvement and autonomy featured highly) – but his philosophy can be hard to apply to modern situations without lapsing into lifestyle blandishment. There's no such problem, however, with a more recent thinker, whose work engaged ferociously with the limitations of all systems – and in particular the inadequacy of science and technology when it came to filling the void once occupied by gods.

Friedrich Nietzsche was a sick man for most of his life, plagued by near-blindness, paralysing migraines, and collapses that kept him bed-bound for weeks. As a result, much of his mature philosophy was written in terse, exalted bursts, inspired by days spent walking in the Alps. In her recent biography of Nietzsche, *I am Dynamite!*, Sue Prideaux describes these oscillations as a form of destruction and renewal.

"Every illness was a death, a dip down into Hades. Every recuperation was a joyful rebirth, a regeneration. This mode of existence refreshed him. *Neuschmecken* ('new-tasting') was his word for it. During each fleeting recuperation the world gleamed anew. And so each recuperation became not only his own rebirth, but also the birth of a whole new world, a new set of problems that demanded new answers."

> Nietzsche insisted that all systems proposing an end to questioning were suspect.

Nietzsche's was a philosophy neither of balance nor harmony, but of creative destruction. He refused answers and resolutions, ending his greatest works with an ellipsis rather than a conclusion. "Philosophy as I have understood and lived it," he wrote in the Foreword to *Ecce Homo*, "is voluntary living in ice and high mountains – a seeking after everything strange and questionable in existence, all that has hitherto been excommunicated by morality."

It was a violently hard existence – and Nietzsche's refusal of answers or fixed positions left rich pickings for those who wished to misrepresent him. Yet, in the works he completed in his own lifetime, Nietzsche insisted that all systems proposing an end to questioning were suspect – with a special ire reserved for those that claimed to do so on the basis of scientific certainty.

What's wrong with wishing to live a balanced life? Nothing, so long as you accept that balance implies measures, priorities, and values, all of which can and must be contested if they are not to be hollowed out. While Silicon Valley may have pioneered life's technological quantification, the apotheosis of today's machine-assisted equilibrium is to be found in China, where state surveillance is working steadily towards ubiquitous assessment: the constant algorithmic counterbalancing of approved and unapproved actions, of patriotic and unpatriotic deeds.

Under this vision of the near future, each citizen will be constantly rated according to a unified social credit score – with every trip, purchase, action or inaction integrated into the edifice of industrially-engineered harmony. The result: harmonious lives within a harmonious nation. It's a fine principle – so long as you're prepared to presuppose its rightness.

When it comes to systems and their automation of our ethics, Aristotle and Nietzsche would have agreed on at least one thing: without the chance fundamentally to debate the weight of both individual and collective actions, any box you put people inside is ultimately a prison. ∎

"If the blood humour is too strong and robust, calm it with balance and harmony."

Xunzi

Photo: Summer, 1939, Fortepan.

Ethical children

Questions from
and answers for children,
by Matthew Beard

***Why do adults work all the time?
Why can't they play half the time too?***

Take a second to imagine your perfect world. How much time do you think everyone – children and adults alike – would spend working and playing? I'm guessing there would be lots less work and lots more play.

Now, think about what we'd need to change in our world to create your perfect world. Tomorrow, if I decided to work half as much as I do, it would be hard for me and my family to keep buying food, living in our house or doing lots of the fun things we love.

When you look at the way our society works, it looks a lot like a world that is built around work. All the things that make our lives really important have to fit in around the time we spend working. If you're really

lucky, you might be able to do something playful – like painting, playing sport or something else that delights you – as work, but for lots of people, that's not the case.

When you look at it that way, it turns out adults don't spend much time playing for the same reasons as you on a really busy day: because there are other things they have to do. If we want to spend more time playing, we would really need to change the world – and that would take work. But all the work is worth it if we get to play at the end of it, right?

***Why do I have to listen to someone if
I know they're wrong?***

I'm not sure you do! There are probably times when it would be bad to listen to someone who you know

is wrong. Let's say someone is saying horrible, bullying lies about you. If you kept listening to them, you'd be doing something bad for your own mental health. It would be better to stop listening (and even better if they stopped telling those horrible lies).

But even though listening can be hurtful, sometimes we can hurt someone by not listening to them. Imagine you have something to say, but someone else thinks you're wrong (maybe an adult isn't listening to you). It's a pretty frustrating feeling isn't it?

That's because being treated like we're not serious thinkers who can come up with good ideas feels disrespectful. We all think we've got something to offer, and we want other people to at least give us a chance to say what we think.

Listening to what someone has to say, even when they're wrong, can also teach us something. We often think about ideas being either totally right or totally wrong, but sometimes they're mixed together.

Listening helps us to see the ideas underneath someone's mistake. That can help us see why they got it wrong and might also help us spot the things they got right as well. N

Ethical dilemma

by Matthew Beard

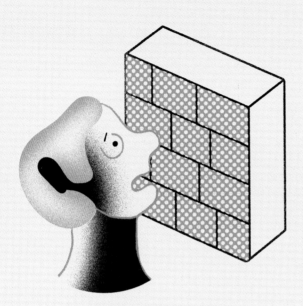

As is the case for most people, I have friends with a range of views on subjects encompassing everything from politics to how to best raise children. I try to be balanced when discussing these subjects with people whose views differ from mine – which becomes more difficult the more the person's views diverge from mine. (Often, they're not so balanced.) But I manage to stay civil, and, without preaching too much, counter their arguments and present my own. We don't have to agree on all topics to remain friends, and I'm aware that there are different ways to interpret any given situation so there's not just one 'right' way of looking at a matter. However, when it comes to the environment – to global warming, to waste, to the extinction of species at the hands of humans, and the destruction of the environment – I am unable to listen to someone who thinks that everything is going along just fine. My question is: do I have to be balanced in my views when I'm certain we are heading in the wrong direction when it comes to how we're treating the Earth? Must I hear out a climate change denialist?

The problem with the metaphor of balance is that truth and evidence are often imbalanced. Only someone who is ignoring a huge part of the story can believe the arguments are balanced on issues like climate change, buying products made by child labour or profiting from war and violence.

To take a 'balanced' view on issues where the weight of evidence is overwhelmingly on one side of the argument seems perverse – after all, the whole point of looking for evidence and thinking through issues is to get to a view we think is 'right'. And in most cases, what's right isn't a question of popularity.

The problem with the 'balanced' approach is it assumes that we haven't yet worked out what's right. In that context, it's not a bad idea to be open to all the available evidence and argument – to engage with it in good faith and see if it makes sense on its own terms and in conjunction with all the other evidence we have.

The English philosopher John Stuart Mill held a similar belief: he thought the reason we shouldn't censor any ideas in a free society is because we should always be humble enough to accept that we might be wrong. Silencing or ignoring certain opinions might mean ignoring the truth – a dangerous proposition.

But Mill also thought listening to other people's ideas could help reassure us that we're right. If our ideas keep holding up despite opposition, we can be pretty sure we've hit on an idea worth taking seriously.

Of course, Mill's 'marketplace of ideas' approach has a huge issue, which climate debates have brought into sharp relief: it doesn't allow bad ideas to die. Anybody can reignite an obviously bad idea, and we're expected to hear it out and defeat it with good ideas – even though we've done so before. That's bad for reaching consensus, and doubly bad when consensus is needed to stop a moral and ecological catastrophe.

Not all ideas are created equal. We owe it to ourselves and each other to protect the best ideas from being corrupted by lies, self-interest or bad reasoning. Sometimes, that might mean hearing someone out in order to correct them – if they're willing to listen. Other times, that might mean engaging in conversations that will actually lead somewhere, rather than shouting at a brick wall. ◻

poet
by **NewPhilosopher**

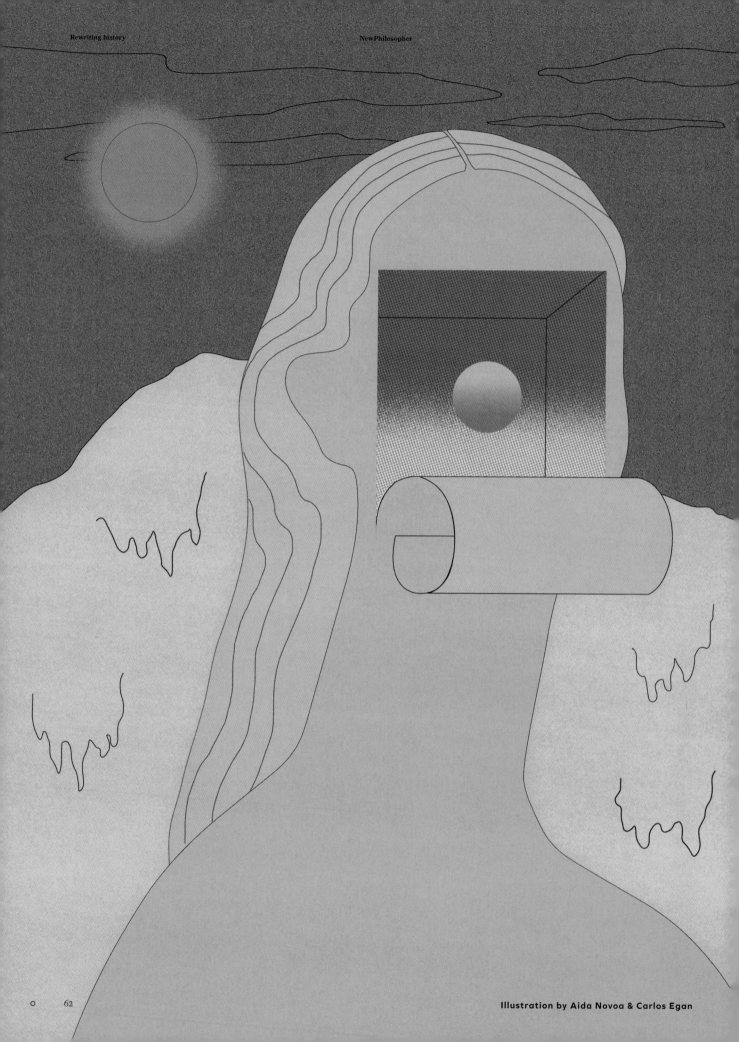

Illustration by Aida Novoa & Carlos Egan

by Tiffany Jenkins

Rewriting history

When the Royal Academy in London announced an upcoming exhibition on the *Renaissance Nude*, the press and commentariat went into overdrive, with a flurry of coverage along the lines of: 'political correctness gone mad'. *The Telegraph* raged: "Royal Academy nudes to have 'gender equality' in new post-#metoo exhibition". The Museums Association, the professional body for the sector, enthused and confirmed: "It is the first time the academy has introduced a gender quota for its exhibitions."

But it wasn't true; there was no quota for the show. Though there were, roughly, as many male nudes as female, achieving equity was not the intention of the curators. The number of men's buttocks was about the same as female bottoms, because that's what the artists of the time painted. Take a peek at Michelangelo's towering sculpture *David* and you will see that the male body was much venerated.

Sloppy journalism and a rush to judge aside, the misunderstanding and overreach was perhaps understandable, and holds a lesson. Because cultural institutions have been falling over themselves to rebalance the artists and paintings in art galleries along more politically acceptable lines. The reporters were following a headline that was set in play by the cultural world, one that could negatively affect our knowledge and appreciation of art history, as well as our understanding of the struggle for women's equality.

In 2018, after the thirty-year long activism of the collective the Guerrilla Girls, whose infamous billboard poster reads: "Do women have to be naked to get into the Met?", Manchester Art Gallery removed from its walls John William Waterhouse's *Hylas and the Nymphs*, depicting naked (female) water nymphs. Postcards of the painting were removed from sale in the shop. The gallery defended the move as an act to "prompt a debate" about which pictures get displayed and by whom. They achieved that, and more, provoking an angry backlash from the public, who love the painting, and don't like being told what they can and cannot look at. The painting has been reinstated, for now.

In recent years, the Uffizi in Florence, home to the greatest art of the Renaissance, has tried to rebalance the gender of its artists, with exhibitions devoted to 'overlooked' female painters: to canonise the 'Old Mistresses', if you like. Elsewhere, the Grand Palais in Paris opened a show for the accomplished French portrait painter of the late 18th century,

Madame Vigée Le Brun, which travelled to the Metropolitan Museum of Art in New York. The show was heralded as being "long overdue". The artist had been disregarded previously, it was suggested, on account of her being female. Along similar lines, in 2016, the Prado in Madrid opened its first solo show of a female artist, the Flemish still life painter Clara Peeters. And when Frances Morris, director of Tate Modern, was appointed in 2016 she criticised the gallery's permanent collection representing 335 female artists compared with 959 male artists as "just not good enough". When it opened a year later, she devoted half of the solo-artist rooms in the Tate Modern extension, Switch House, to female artists, including Ana Lupas, Louise Bourgeois, and Suzanne Lacy.

There are legitimate instances of fine women painters being forgotten, and no doubt those artists with exhibitions warranted them. Ten years ago, not many people had heard of the Belgian Baroque artist, Michaelina Wautier. Since her first retrospective last year, at Rubens House and the MAS, in Antwerp, she is being reconsidered as one of the finest painters of her time. That is as it should be.

But Wautier wasn't unknown in her time, she just became so over time, a forgetting was as likely to be down to the vagaries of fashion, as much as her gender, something many male artists know quite a bit about. Take Johannes Vermeer: this wonderful painter of the ideal domestic life is now a household name, spoken of in reverential terms. But he was only modestly successful, barely known, and poor when he died. And then there is Rembrandt. When the master of the self-portrait died, he was given a pauper's funeral. Though

he was successful early on in his career, his fortunes plummeted. He fell out of favour, made detractors, and was buried in an unknown grave in the Westerkerk.

Even if it is just to liven things up and to refresh our eyes, I am all for changing who is in favour and who is out. Tastes, after all, change. But in the main, the great women artists currently enjoying their time in the spot-

The rewriting of the artistic canon to include more women can distort it to breaking point.

light, including Madame Vigée Le Brun and Artemisia Gentileschi, were, in their time, celebrated and widely appreciated; the former was much favoured by Marie Antoinette. Finding other artists to shoehorn into the category of great, because they were female, is more difficult. Because they were not there in the first place.

The problem is that art history, and, indeed society, is not fair. No amount of rummaging around in the store cupboards of history is going to change that. You aren't going to make the visitor adore Barbara Longhi, a once-admired Renaissance painter, because she isn't good enough. She doesn't stand the test of time. You can add Clara Peeters and Louise Moillon to the canon, but because they are really fine painters, regardless of their sex.

Canons are flexible. They can and should be challenged and reshaped. But so often with feminist art history, what you see is a cynical disregard for the achievement of great artists, and a failure to understand and recognise

why women did not reach the same great heights.

For hundreds of years women were considered unequal to men and were confined to the private sphere. That is why there have been comparatively fewer great women artists. Not because they were overlooked, but because of their place in society, because of low expectations and lack of opportunity. That is also why, when they did break out of those norms, do their own thing, and excelled at it, their work is so exciting. Michaelina Wautier's *The Triumph of Bacchus* is a work of sensual power, made all the more impressive by the fact that it was painted more than 200 years before most women were permitted to attend life drawing classes. But even then, I doubt she would have appreciated being lauded for her biology rather than her artistic ability.

The rewriting of the artistic canon to include more women can distort it to breaking point. The Sonia Delaunay exhibition at Tate Modern a few years ago was good, but her excellent work didn't justify the scale of the show nor the claims made for it. As a visitor, I left cynical, thinking that too much positive discrimination was at work, and wondering if this institutional act of rebalancing didn't throw the rest of its curatorial expertise into question.

Which brings us back to the reaction to the RA *Renaissance Nude* exhibition. Once collections are deemed to be run on the basis of politics, on what we would like to see, rather than what was, the eye becomes distrustful, even suspicious. Genuine and original scholarship can be brushed aside and dismissed as the work of political correctness. When in fact the RA show was simply uncovering the way the male nude was once put on a pedestal. ◨

"He knows to live who keeps the middle state,
And neither leans on this side nor on that."

Alexander Pope

Acrobat, Mexico, Xochipala, 900-500 BCE, LA County Museum of Art.

Dayt

Night

ime*

-time

Daytime* = 12 hours and 7 minutes
Night-time = 11 hours and 53 minutes

*Daytime being the period of the day during which any given point on Earth experiences natural illumination from direct sunlight.

by Timothy Olds

Goldilocks day

Photo: *Hergé Countdown*, by Bert Kaufmann

There's nothing more democratic than time. Donald Trump and Hillary Clinton, Bill Gates and the Dalai Lama, Usain Bolt and Serena Williams all have exactly 1,440 minutes in their day, and the rip of time sweeps us all towards the future at exactly 60 minutes per hour.

Imagine this: you decide you need to get fit, so you determine to go swimming for half an hour each day. You need to find time to get into your swimmers, get to the pool, do your workout, get home, have a shower and get changed. Let's say an hour all up. Where does the time come from? It's not magicked out of nothing. Time, like water, is incompressible and inextensible. You could get up earlier or go to bed later, skive off work a little earlier, have a shorter shower, skip some social media time, forego intimacy with your beloved, get some takeaway instead of cooking. What would you do? What do people actually do?

I know the answer because a few years ago we did a little research project. We got 100 people and asked two-thirds of them to start an exercise program, in their own time, requiring either two-and-a-half or five hours a week. The other third were told to just live their lives as usual.

We compared changes in time use between the two groups. So, where did the time come from?

It turns out that the extra hours came from the three deep time reservoirs of modern life: TV, sleep, and household chores. When they needed to squeeze out some extra minutes and hours, our participants slept less, watched less TV, and let the house go to rack and ruin. Unfortunately, at the end of the seven-week program, their time use flowed back to exactly what it was before: when we have time on our hands, we catch up on sleep and TV, and put the house back in order. The tidal drag of routine eventually pulls us back into our quotidian rhythms.

And so we are constantly ballasting bits of time against others, trying to balance our lives. We're told to get 8 hours' sleep, at least 30 minutes of physical activity and not to spend too much time sitting down. The problem is this: if you do more of one thing, you have to do less of another. If I decide to sleep an extra hour, something has to go. What should I sacrifice? Physical activity? TV? Socialising? And what's the temporal exchange rate? To get the same reduction in depression, for example, as I would get from 30 minutes walking each day, how much extra sleep would I need? How much less time would I have to spend watching TV?

Retirement is a nice life stage to study this, because one day you wake up and no longer have to go to work. You feel like you're jetsam on the banks of the river of time. How do you fill up the empty hours? It turns out that you fill them up with about 40 minutes more sleep, 40 minutes more TV and an hour's more chores – those time reservoirs again – plus a little extra reading and socialising. We measured 100 older adults from six months before retirement to a year after, and had a look at how changes in their time use predicted changes in their mental health and well-being. Filling up the empty hours with either more physical activity or more sleep was universally beneficial. But the exchange rate between sleep and physical activity was different depending on which aspect of mental health you were looking at. For overall well-being an extra 45 minutes of sleep was as good as 60 minutes of walking. I'll take the sleep, thanks. But for stress, you need to sleep an extra two-and-a-half hours to get the same benefit as just 20 minutes of walking. Easier to walk.

The big question is: What's the best balance, just the right mix for health and well-being, not too much and not too little of anything? What's the right trade-off? What's the Goldilocks Day?

We have some clues about this, too. We measured how 1,000 11-year-old kids and their parents used their time over a number of days, using activity trackers on their wrists and 24-hour recalls. We measured every aspect of their health and well-being. We took so much blood, tissue, hair, urine, faeces, and fingernail clippings that they left the lab a couple of kilos lighter. We measured blood pressure, blood glucose, blood lipids, kidney function, liver function, immune function, body fat, hearing, quality of life, biological

> We seem to live in a world of liquid time, where we can trade off the present against the future.

age, literacy, numeracy… and then we asked what mix of activities predicted the best possible health.

It turns out that the Goldilocks Day is pretty much the same for almost all those different health outcomes, from quality of life to blood pressure. For adults, the best mix is 6-9 hours of sleep, no more than 7 hours of sitting, and 9-12 hours either standing or moving. Kids have it much easier: the Goldilocks Day is 8.5-11.5 hours of sleep, no more than 8 hours sitting, and 5-7 hours standing or moving. With kids, however, there is a catch. For the best results in school, the best day is 11-14 hours sitting and only 1-2 hours of standing or moving. So there are time trade-offs here, too. In 15-year-old boys, the best amount of sleep for academic performance is

seven and three-quarter hours. For mental health it is eight and three-quarter hours. What do you want your son to be: an A-grade student who is depressed, or a B-grade student who is happy?

You would think that the fluidity of the modern world would make these trade-offs a bit easier. We are no longer tied to the iron regimen of TV schedules or the workplace. We can defer our TV viewing for whenever we like. We can work at home, in the evenings or on the weekend. We can do our shopping online. We seem to live in a world of liquid time, where we can trade off the present against the future. But we're all carried along by the ebbs and flows of the river of time, and no amount of revolutionaries shooting the clocks, creating new calendars or declaring Year Zero will change that. Time is a Möbius strip, where sacrifices blend imperceptibly into compensations. We're always running out of time, and time is slipping away. All we can do is to sit and stare out over the infinite horizons of the great ocean of time, and do our best to manage it. ◘

"Believe me, wise men don't say 'I shall live to do that', tomorrow's life is too late; live today."

Martial

BALANCE

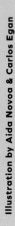

Illustration by Aida Novoa & Carlos Egan

balance

/ˈbal(ə)ns/

noun:

1. An even distribution of weight enabling someone or something to remain upright and steady.
2. A situation in which different elements are equal or in the correct proportions.
3. Mental or emotional stability.
4. (Art) Harmony of design and proportion.
5. An apparatus for weighing, especially one with a central pivot, beam, and two scales.
6. Counteracting weight or force.
7. Figure representing the difference between credits and debits in an account.

verb:

1. In a steady position so that it does not fall.
2. Offset or compare the value of (one thing) with another.
3. Compare debits and credits in (an account) so as to ensure that they are equal.

Origin: Middle English (in balance (in the sense of weighing)): from Old French *balance* (noun), *balancer* (verb), based on late Latin (libra) *bilanx* '(balance) having two scale pans', from *bi-* 'twice, having two' + *lanx* 'scale pan'.

Source:
Oxford English Dictionary

Building an equal society

Interviewee: Elizabeth Anderson
Interview by Alex Hinds

Alex Hinds: Balance is a topic that you have touched on in your work across political philosophy, law, feminist epistemology, and egalitarianism – and in particular, in your forthcoming book on the history of egalitarianism.

Elizabeth Anderson: Balance plays a really important role in moral and political philosophy, both in terms of methodology and in terms of the substantive content of moral requirements.

If we think about methodology, we have this notion of 'reflective equilibrium.' This is the idea that in trying to figure out what is right or just, we seek an equilibrium between intuitive, general propositions or principles about right and wrong and our intuitions about particular cases. We move back and forth; we refine the principles against our intuitions about cases and try and find principles that will fit all the particular cases; and then we also seek new cases and try to get them in equilibrium with our principles. We pretty much settle on the moral view

that is in equilibrium between our intuitions about particular cases and our intuitions about general principles that could explain those cases. That's a really interesting methodological view that involves the notion of balance. One way to cash out that view is through a mode of theorising about justice that's known as *social contract theory*. Social contract theory says that the principles of justice are whatever principles rational people, standing in relations of equality to one another, would freely and voluntarily consent to be governed by. That also has a kind of equilibrium notion built into it, because any principle of justice is founded on an idea of reciprocity – "I will go along with this principle if you also go along." The outcome of our discussion of what we're all willing to go along with, conditional on other people going along, is also a kind of equilibrium. Many theorists working through social contract theory believe that if you start off with everyone situated in a symmetrical position (no one under anyone else's thumb, no one forced or subordinated to just make concessions to somebody else), that everyone will expect that the principles of justice would treat them as an equal – neither superior or inferior to anyone else.

So, all of these notions of equilibrium generally tend in an egalitarian direction, into a vision substantively that justice involves something like 'whatever principles would support a free society of equals and make such a society possible'.

That was actually going to be the very first question here – starting with those basics – what are we talking about when we talk about egalitarianism? What are its basic foundational principles or ideas, and where do we see them at play in society?

Right, exactly. From a social contract perspective, people are going to think, "Well, I don't want to be subordinate". Now maybe different people might think, "Well, I'd like to be superior to others." But there's a wonderful anthropologist, Christopher Boehm, who wrote a book called *Hierarchy in the Forest*. He went around and investigated how hunter-gatherer peoples think about equality. One thing we know about hunter-gatherer peoples, from the anthropological literature, is that they are uniformly egalitarian. We also know from the archaeological record and the record of fossils of human ancestors and so forth, that we all evolved in hunter-gatherer conditions.

Illustration by Alvaro Hidalgo

Elizabeth Anderson is Arthur F. Thurnau Professor and John Dewey Distinguished University Professor of Philosophy and Women's Studies, Chair of the Department of Philosophy at University of Michigan, and the former President of the Central Division of the American Philosophical Association.

We all started off, the human species started off, as hunter-gatherers. Now we don't know *precisely* that our ancestors, as hunter-gatherers were equally egalitarian as present hunter-gatherers. But the sheer universality of egalitarianism among widely dispersed hunter-gatherer groups is certainly suggestive that that's a kind of natural equilibrium that hunter-gatherers tend to converge on. One reason for that is that if you are mobile, moving around all the time, you can't really afford to be lugging a lot of stuff along with you. So inequality of wealth really doesn't make very much sense: you want to be travelling lightly.

So even in terms of hunting, if you decide to keep a carcass all to yourself, you can't eat all of it or move it around with you, so it's not a big advantage to have all the resources and wealth in that sort of situation.

In fact, to the contrary, it's a disadvantage. We also know uniformly across all hunter-gatherer groups that meat is shared, and that affords a kind of insurance policy. It's kind of the hunter-gatherer version of social insurance – if my spear doesn't kill the big carcass this week, somebody else's will and they have to share, and next week maybe it's my turn to be lucky at the hunt, and then I will share. That's a kind of early version of social insurance. We do the same with unemployment insurance, and with old age insurance and so forth, because after a while you get old enough and you're not really that great a hunter or maybe you can't hunt at all anymore. Hunter-

gatherers take care of their own, just like in modern societies.

Now when I think about egalitarianism, the first thing that comes to my mind are notions of equality, fairness and justice. Am I correct in making these sorts of connections, or are there some really important differences and distinctions to be drawn here?

Among contemporary theorists, some basal notion of equality of human beings is taken for granted. We are all equally entitled to human rights, no one is born in subjection to another as a matter of right or destiny. But within that basic egalitarianism of rights and liberties, most theorists think that some inequalities can emerge out of that with justification. That, I think, tends to the reality that to have a prosperous society we have all kinds of organisations of team production, and those organisations contain an internal hierarchy of offices. So, if I think about my university, there's a president, there are deans, there are chairs of departments – I am a chair of a department – right? So you do have a kind of hierarchy there, and it's very difficult to imagine how to pull off complex team production (as we see in education, healthcare, mass transportation and all kinds of industries) without some kind of hierarchy of offices.

Egalitarianism in a modern, complex world is not *strict* in the way that it could be among hunter-gatherers because we have a division of labour, whereas hunter-gatherers pretty much do all the things that their group needs. There's a primitive gen-

der division of labour, but even that in some hunter-gatherer groups is not very strict.

With the hierarchy of offices, most egalitarians say, "Okay, so there will be differential powers and to a certain degree differential esteem attaching to the higher offices." But we at least need equality of opportunity for people to attain higher offices. And everyone getting a decent shot at developing their talents and competing for those offices.

There has been renewed debate recently about equality of opportunity vs. equality of outcome and the perceived tensions between freedom and equality here. What are we to do in trying to strike the right balance here? How far should we go in our efforts to address and rebalance the world's inequalities?

That's a really great question. I do think that in the past 50 years or so we have seen steadily increasing inequality within the rich countries of the world, and 'within-country' inequality in general has been increasing. Once-poor countries are now attaining middle-income – China being most prominent, but India is getting there as well – we're also seeing increasing 'within-country' inequality, although the extraordinary growth of China and India means that inequality has actually been dropping a bit if you compare people across the world. But that is mostly powered by economic development in two very, very large countries (China and India).

But within a society, that is, within a State, inequality has been rising

This argument that incentives are needed to stimulate production has been carried to extremes that go far beyond what the difference principle would permit.

in most countries of the world, and that is certainly a matter of concern. One reason for that is, as we see in politics, when we have huge inequalities the rich start calling all of the political shots much more than they used to. There has always been some imbalance there in terms of political influence. But now it's quite extreme.

So right now, in the 21st century, is a particular bad time? And we are seeing an increase in that sort of inequality in terms of wealth and subsequently, political power?

Yes. So just to give you an illustration, corporate power is at unprecedented heights in the post-World War II era, whereas it used to be balanced by the power of organised labour. But organised labour across the rich countries has been in decline for about 40 to 50 years. So there isn't really any countervailing power. Especially with the World Trade Organization and other trade agreements, corporations can call all the shots because they can move the money instantly, shut down factories and open them up somewhere else, which has really eroded the bargaining power of workers and altered the distribution of income towards capital owners and against people who are working for a living.

On the topic of wealth and economic equality, how are we to think about wealth in egalitarian terms? You've said before that complete economic equality is incompatible not just with freedom, but with equality itself – could you expand on that idea a little bit for us?

Yes. If you look at what kind of political structure is needed to achieve absolutely strict, material equality, it requires massive State repression to get there – Mao's China is a good model to look at in that regard, as they tried to do that for a while. And the difficulty is that if you have massive

State repression it means that you need political power tightly concentrated in the hands of a single party, telling everybody else what to do and what they can't do. That's a type of inequality too.

Consider what it takes to get pure, material inequality, as soon as you get a surplus in society. This happens as soon as you are beyond the level of economic development of hunter-gatherers – who are basically at subsistence, so they're all equal materially because they don't really have any surplus. Once you get a surplus it's very difficult to have *absolute* equal sharing of that surplus without some kind of concentrated State power that's telling people they can't do a lot of stuff, which is in itself a kind of inequality. So you get material equality arising out of political inequality. See, that is really the difficulty here.

Pure, perfect equality along all dimensions really isn't feasible. But you can get close. After the Bolshevik revolution in Russia they tried to establish equal wages for everyone. Mao tried to do that too. What they found was that some people continued to work hard, and other people just laid back and let the hard workers do the hard work. Not only did that result in a collapse of production, and hence of wealth for the whole society, but it also created a lot of resentment because the hard-workers are thinking, "These other people are just free-riding off our effort!". So in both Mao's agricultural communes and under Lenin, they realised that they did need to introduce some incentives to reward people who worked harder than others. That introduced material inequality. Incentives then, I think, are justified because they lift all. You have higher economic growth, there's more to share around through social insurance and things like that. So some degree of material inequality, I think, is tolerable.

John Rawls advanced a very interesting principle designed to permit some degree of material inequality, but to limit it. His principle is called the 'difference principle'. It basically says, "We should allow inequality of income and wealth only to the extent that it maximises the economic prospects of the least advantaged group." The least advantaged would want that, because that makes them absolutely better off, and the more advantaged would get more, so they're okay. Rawls thought that this agreement on permissible inequality would be something that people in a social contract would accept.

To take business for an example, we might see businesses and business owners, as part of an advantaged group, making profits for themselves at the top end while also maximising the economic prospects of more disadvantaged groups through providing both employment and economic stimulus and growth for the broader community. Is that the idea?

Correct, exactly. Now, here's the trick. This argument that incentives are needed to stimulate production has been carried to extremes that go far beyond what the difference principle would permit. If you look at executive compensation for example, you are promised many, many millions of dollars if you hit some profit figure for the year. What that actually encourages executives to do is to take enormous risks with the corporation in order to hit that target, because there's really no downside to failure. If anything, it encourages excessively risky behaviour that's not even good from an efficiency point of view.

Stepping back and looking from a sociological point of view, we find that back in the '50s, CEO's of the leading corporations were quite content with vastly lower compensation than they currently get. One of the things I love to give my students just to get them

If we look deeply into human history, we find that the first group-based inequality that arises is gender inequality.

thinking about historical perspective is a wonderful article that came out, I think it was in *Forbes* magazine somewhere around 1955, where they interview a CEO of a big insurance firm in Connecticut. They go to his house and they talk about what he enjoys. Lo and behold, he has a *two-car garage.* For vacation, he has a little boat and he goes fishing. The CEO of a major, Fortune 500 corporation, basically lived what today we would recognise as an upper-middle class lifestyle. I did a consumer price index deflation calculation on his salary, and it's equivalent of about USD$400,000 a year today. This is definitely on the high end of US salaries for ordinary salaried workers, but far below what people in the C-Suite get today. It doesn't seem that you need outsized incentives to motivate people. Even the most talented can be content with a lot less than what they're currently paid.

Now as I understand it, you are currently working on a book about the history of egalitarianism. Where do we find the origins of egalitarian ideas and ideals, and how have they changed over time?

The anthropologists tell us that they've been with us from the start. Hunter-gatherers are pretty sophisticated political theorists. Christopher Boehm quotes one of them doing his own spontaneous political philosophy, explaining why their band treats everyone as equals. He says something like, "Everyone would like to be superior to the others, but they know they can't get that, so they agree to be equals." It's an excellent social contract perspective that he was articulating. That's the equilibrium point that everyone agrees on, and so they settle on that and are fine with it. This idea is very, very ancient and goes deep into our psyche.

The real question is actually, "How does inequality arise?". Most people think that the prime driver of inequality is State formation. You can't really have a State unless the economy is producing a surplus. Then the rulers are basically seizing the surplus for themselves. The State starts off not being all that great a thing for people. Then what you find is that people get locked in to inequality because States have overwhelming concentrated power and can wipe out the egalitarian hunter-gatherers and tribal societies with overwhelming military might. They conquer most of the world and then we seem to be locked into a state of inequality.

How do we get out of that?

Well, that's what democracy is all about. People have to come to recognise that the power of the State is itself contingent on the willingness of the people to obey the political leaders. If enough people decide that they're sick of this and that their leader is abusive, and that they can manage to organise themselves to resist and maybe make demands for individual rights, equitable sharing and things like that, we have the origins of democracy. This is a way to move towards an egalitarian

society, but now large scale, complex, State-based, and with a sophisticated division of labour.

As a really good example of this idea of the power of the people in rebalancing inequalities, one particular movement that I'm sure you have a lot to say about as a professor not just of Philosophy but also of Women's Studies, is the feminist movement. How does feminism relate to these egalitarian ideas around balance, justice and equality?

This is a fabulous question, because if we look deeply into human history, we find that the first group-based inequality that arises is gender inequality. Even hunter-gatherers vary a lot in terms of how equal women are. Some of them are quite gender-egalitarian. But in some you see pretty high degrees of domestic violence that seems to be connected to a primitive gender division of labour. Women are taking care of the kids, which makes them vulnerable in various ways – they're not bringing in the meat, for example, because they're spending their time taking care of the kids.

With gender inequality being the first group-based inequality to emerge, it takes a really, really long time for feminism to arise and for women to be able to organise *as women* and demand equal rights. Historically, we see feminism arising in Europe at least around the 17th century. Women start speaking for themselves. Partly, this has to do with a burst of literacy, where people including women learn how to read. Learning how to read is a really formative thing and gives people power. It gives them access to knowledge, communication, the ability to organise, share ideas, and allows people to think for themselves more confidently than if they can't read. Once women start thinking for themselves and communicating among themselves, then they can get together and make demands.

The key to all egalitarianism is that the subordinate groups need to exercise solidarity and collective action – that is how you make egalitarian progress.

As we've discussed here, if equality is the foundation of egalitarianism, should we endeavour to treat everybody in exactly the same way? Or are there real risks in taking such a literal approach to equality, such as failing to account for natural human diversity?

Yes, we cannot treat everyone in *exactly* the same way. People differ along any number of dimensions that call for differential treatment. Take age for instance – you can't treat children like adults, because that wouldn't be good for them, and of course we also have to make accommodations for people with disabilities and things like that. So I don't think identical treatment is a good model for thinking about equality. One way of thinking about it is in terms of equal respect – you can accord everyone a basic sense of dignity and also recognise their equal standing to make claims on one's own behaviour. If you are making decisions that have an impact on their interests, then their interests should stand equally with other people's interests. That way of thinking is consistent with recognising that, for instance, within an organisation with a division of labour, different people are going to have different tasks assigned to them on account of their occupation and skills and so forth. There's nothing wrong with that. You just need that for team production.

In thinking about these egalitarian ideas, I'm sure it would seem to most people that equality is obviously a good thing… but is that always the case? Is inequality always a bad thing, or are there circumstances where it is acceptable, or even desirable?

I do want to say a few things *against* meritocracy. We live in an age that pretends it's meritocratic – that everyone in a superior position has attained that position in virtue of their own talent. I think it's arrant nonsense. Those people who are lucky enough to have highly-privileged parents who could send them to fancy schools are getting those positions by and large, so I'm not a fan of meritocracy. Even if in the first generation you could place everyone into jobs purely based on their ability to perform those jobs, in the next generation those people who held higher jobs that required more education or esteem are going to pass that advantage onto their kids. It's not an accident that you see, for instance, that actors often have parents who are actors or that the children of doctors are more likely to be doctors and so forth, because there's an insider's path for almost every profession. The idea of meritocracy isn't actually realisable.

What we want then, from an egalitarian point of view, is to open up opportunities for disruption of the intergenerational transmission of privilege. That requires opening a lot of alternative paths to success, especially moving very, very vigorously against attempts by parents to buy privilege for their kids. You may have seen the admissions scandal that has been rocking the elite colleges of the United States. By meritocratic standards this is utterly scandalous, but in a way it's utterly predictable too – this is what parents do for their kids!

Equality has come quite a long way in the past few centuries, and in the 21st century it appears that we are making real inroads into some of its most pressing problems – such as slavery, racism, and women's rights. But do we still live in a world that remains out of balance, where inequality is truly thriving? And are these problems to be solved, or battles that will be constantly waged?

It does indeed, yes, because the people at the top want to monopolise opportunities. They want to hoard them for themselves and for their group. So generally, we find that the emergence of distinct, social group identities (which could be along any number of lines – race, ethnicity, religion, caste, and of course gender) is powered a lot by inequality, and by the desire of more privileged groups to hoard opportunities for themselves and not share them with others.

One way to do that is to sharpen up a sense of one's own distinctive social identity and draw sharp boundaries between one's identity and other identities. In that sense, inequality powers identity politics. But also of course, once hierarchies are structured around these kinds of identities then the subordinate groups, the disadvantaged groups, need to rally around their own identities just in order to defend themselves and in order to move forward. We see identity politics on both sides – but it always starts from the top.

It seems like a strange irony that the solution to inequalities arising out of identity politics and the formation of distinct in-groups and out-groups might just be for the disadvantaged groups to more sharply define and tighten up their own group identities.

Sometimes you have to fight fire with fire. From an egalitarian point of view, however, that is only a strategy, not a final end point. The aim is not to set the whole world on fire, but to put out the fire.

What Martin Luther King, Jr. called the "beloved community" involves coming together in full recognition of our common humanity. Oppressed groups need to organise themselves for self-defence. But every democratic social movement has also forged alliances and joined with other groups to build a more equal society. That is a collective project for all of us. ◼

Politics and gender balance

Although it's the highest percentage in history, fewer than 15 per cent of countries or territories are ruled by women. The majority of countries have never elected a female leader.

Countries that have never elected a female leader include:

USA	Syria
Iran	Papua New Guinea
Russia	Japan
Saudi Arabia	Hungary
Greece	Morocco
South Africa	Ethiopia
Mexico	Italy
Sweden	The Netherlands
Spain	Belgium
Egypt	France

Number of countries that have had female heads of government around the world:

Up to 1960: 0
1960-present: 60+

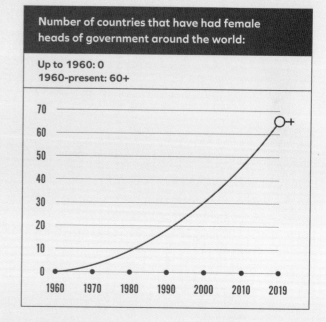

First female heads of government

1960s

Where: Sri Lanka
Who: Sirimavo Bandaranaike
When: 21 July 1960
How long: 4 years, 249 days

Where: India
Who: Indira Gandhi
When: 24 January 1966
How long: 11 years, 90 days

Where: Israel
Who: Golda Meir
When: 17 March 1969
How long: 5 years, 78 days

1970s

Where: Argentina
Who: Isabel Perón
When: 1 July 1974
How long: 1 year, 267 days

Where: Portugal
Who: Maria de Lourdes Pintasilgo
When: 1 August 1979
How long: 186 days

Where: United Kingdom
Who: Margaret Thatcher
When: 4 May 1979
How long: 11 years, 208 days

Also in the 1970s:
Bolivia (Lidia Guelier Tejada, 1979).

Also in the 1980s:
Dominica (Eugenia Charles, 1980), Yugoslavia (Milka Planinc, 1982).

Also in the 1990s:
Lithuania (Kazimira Prunskienė, 1990), Haiti (Ertha Pascal-Trouillot, 1990), Bangladesh (Khaleda Zia, 1991), Burundi (Sylvie Kinigi, 1993), Guyana (Janet Jagan, 1997), Panama (Mireya Moscoso, 1999).

1980s

Where: Norway
Who: Gro Harlem Brundtland
When: 4 February 1981
How long: 252 days

Where: Philippines
Who: Corazon Aquino
When: 25 February 1986
How long: 6 years, 126 days

Where: Pakistan
Who: Benazir Bhutto
When: 2 December 1988
How long: 1 year, 216 days

1990s

Where: Nicaragua
Who: Violeta Chamorro
When: 25 April 1990
How long: 6 years, 260 days

Where: Canada
Who: Kim Campbell
When: 25 June 1993
How long: 132 days

Where: New Zealand
Who: Jenny Shipley
When: 5 December 1997
How long: 2 years, 0 days

2000s

Where: Indonesia
Who: Megawati Sukarnoputri
When: 23 July 2001
How long: 3 years, 89 days

Where: Germany
Who: Angela Merkel
When: 22 November 2005
How long: 13+ years (incumbent)

Where: Chile
Who: Michelle Bachelet
When: 11 March 2006
How long: 4 years, 0 days

2010s

Where: Australia
Who: Julia Gillard
When: 24 June 2010
How long: 3 years, 3 days

Where: Thailand
Who: Yingluck Shinawatra
When: 3 July 2011
How long: 2 years, 308 days

Where: Serbia
Who: Ana Brnabić
When: 29 June 2017
How long: 2+ years (incumbent)

Also in the 2000s:
Finland (Anneli Jäätteenmäki, 2003), Macedonia (Radmila Šekerinska, 2004), Mozambique (Luísa Diogo, 2004), Ukraine (Yulia Tymoshenko, 2005), Jamaica (Portia Simpson-Miller, 2006), Liberia (Ellen Johnson Sirleaf, 2006), South Korea (Han Myung-sook, 2006), Moldova (Zinaida Greceanîi, 2008), Croatia (Jadranka Kosor, 2009), Madagascar (Cécile Manorohanta, 2009).

Also in the 2010s:
Costa Rica (Laura Chinchilla, 2010), Kyrgyzstan (Roza Otunbayeva, 2010), Slovakia (Iveta Radičová, 2010), Trinidad and Tobago (Kamla Persad-Bissessar, 2010), Brazil (Dilma Rousseff, 2011), Denmark (Helle Thorning-Schmidt, 2011), Kosovo (Atifete Jahjaga, 2011), Mali (Cissé Mariam Kaïdama Sidibé, 2011), Malawi (Joyce Banda, 2012), Slovenia (Alenka Bratušek, 2013), Greenland (Aleqa Hammond, 2013), Latvia (Laimdota Straujuma, 2014), Mauritius (Ameenah Firdaus Gurib-Fakim, 2015), Namibia (Saara Kuugongelwa-Amadhila, 2015), Nepal (Bidhya Devi Bhandari , 2015), Estonia (Kersti Kaljulaid, 2016), Marshall Islands (Hilda Heine, 2016), Myanmar (Aung San Suu Kyi, 2016), Taiwan (Tsai Ing-wen, 2016), Romania (Viorica Dăncilă, 2018), Barbados (Mia Mottley, 2018).

Illustration by Aida Novoa & Carlos Egan

by André Dao

Beyond the veil of ignorance

Click on almost any article about the justice system, or step into just about any higher court of law, and you're bound to see the same image: a blindfolded woman, holding a pair of scales in her outstretched hand. Lady Justice (Iustitia if you're an Ancient Roman, Themis or Dike if you're an Ancient Greek) has come to represent many of our common-sense intuitions about what justice is, or should be: impartial, balanced – in a word, fair.

Indeed, the ubiquity of this image suggests that the link between justice and fairness is uncontroversial. But that belies a long-running suspicion that justice is nothing more than a game run by the powerful to subjugate the rest of us. What passes for justice, say the cynics, is just a set of rules designed to rig the system in favour of the rule-makers.

Or as Thrasymachus says in Plato's *Republic*, justice is "nothing other than the interest of the stronger".

To allay the suggestion that Lady Justice's scales are merely ornamental, we might have to turn to her other prop, the blindfold (or, indeed, upgrade the blindfold for a philosophical veil). As 20th century philosopher John Rawls argued, for our conception of justice to remain balanced – unswayed towards those born into genetic, economic or social privilege – we need to think about justice from behind a "veil of ignorance". Specifically, said Rawls, a just society would be the one designed by free and rational persons in a hypothetical "original position", in which all are equal and no one knows what their eventual position in society will be. In fact, behind the veil of ignorance, we hardly know anything about ourselves at all – not what our political or personal preferences will be, nor our natural assets and abilities, like intelligence and strength.

Thus blindfolded, we would – at least according to Rawls – choose two principles to structure our just society: first, that there be equality in the assignment of basic rights and duties, like freedom of speech and the right to vote. Second, that social and economic inequalities are just only if they relate to offices and positions that are open to all under conditions of fair equality of opportunity – which basically means that being born poor shouldn't curb your educational or economic opportunities, at least as compared with a similarly talented and motivated wealthy person.

So far, so balanced – if we only read Rawls this far, then we could imagine that Lady Justice's scales only come out when we're born, to make sure that we're equally endowed with political rights and have access to equal opportunities according to our talents. But Rawls's second principle of justice has a second part: that social and economic inequalities are only just if they result in compensating benefits for everyone, especially the most disadvantaged members of society.

This is where things get interesting – and complicated. The "difference principle", as Rawls calls it, means that the simplest conception of a 'balanced' society – a strictly egalitarian one in which everyone has the same share of the economic pie – isn't necessarily the most just. Instead, justice allows for people's differing talents and motivations to be used to benefit everyone. In other words, our pie shares can be unequal, as long as the whole pie is so big that the smallest share is still larger than in any other social arrangement, including the egalitarian one.

Though tolerant of inequality, the purported moral advantage of the difference principle is that it engenders a sense of social cohesion, because the economic system is ultimately working in everyone's benefit. As Rawls said, "in justice as fairness [people] agree to share one another's fate".

If all this sounds familiar, it's probably because we hear a version of that argument all the time, whenever a politician or a commentator talks about the universal benefits of economic growth. We hear it, for example, being used to justify the enormous salaries of CEOs, or the huge profits of multinational corporations: it's only by lavishly rewarding the talented moneymakers, the argument goes, that we can grow the pie for everyone.

Not that it's only trickle-down economists making this argument. Rawls's theory of justice mirrors a division made in international human rights law, where civil and political rights – analogous to Rawls's basic rights and duties – are considered the 'first generation' of human rights, and subject to strict observance. In contrast, social and economic rights – 'second generation' rights – are subject only to 'progressive realisation', taking into account the economic resources of each government.

The result of this split, as legal historian Samuel Moyn has pointed out, is that since the 1970s the human rights movement has lost any egalitarian spirit it once had: economic and social rights are interpreted as requiring minimum standards, rather than addressing inequality as such. The proof, according to Moyn, is in the numbers. While the last four decades has seen unprecedented poverty alleviation around the world, we've also seen inequality skyrocket.

Well, you might ask – so what? Perhaps Rawls was right, and there's nothing intrinsically morally wrong about inequality, so long as the poorest really are better off. Maybe Lady Justice's scales are a red herring. But a quick look at the rise of populism in democracies around the world is a reminder that inequality is far from being irrelevant to justice. At the very least, Rawls's argument that the difference principle is sufficient to maintain social unity seems to be at odds with a world in which economic inequality seems to be the driving force of disenfranchisement and contestation in the world today. In short, even if the least advantaged are technically better off over the years, extreme inequality – of the kind diagnosed by Thomas Piketty – tears at the social fabric.

Which is why some human rights experts, like Philip Alston, the UN Special Rapporteur on Extreme Poverty and Human Rights, have been pushing back against the marginalisation of so-called second generation economic and social rights. While the traditional human rights approach has been to steer clear of thorny issues like taxation, Alston has been clear that fiscal policies – indeed, any governmental policies that affect the potential redistribution of wealth – are critically relevant to human rights.

There's a reason, after all, that Lady Justice and her scales are so ubiquitous. And it's not just because, as Thrasymachus would have it, the powers that be find the idea of justice a handy fig leaf for their domination. It's because balance – including some kind of economic equality – is critical to most people's sense of justice. Amid ongoing political upheaval in the west, it's a point worth remembering for those who dismiss inequality as a problem in itself. ◼

Even if the least advantaged are technically better off over the years, extreme inequality tears at the social fabric.

"Justice and power must be brought together, so that whatever is just may be powerful, and whatever is powerful may be just."

Blaise Pascal

Illustration: *Arbitration is the true balance of power*, by Joseph Ferdinand Keppler, 1886, LOC.

Photo: *The Bull Leaper*, Knossos, Greece

Balance

The Teacher

Confucius
551–479BCE

The doctrine of the mean

What Heaven has conferred is called The Nature; an accordance with this nature is called The Path of duty; the regulation of this path is called Instruction. The path may not be left for an instant. If it could be left, it would not be the path. On this account, the superior man does not wait till he sees things, to be cautious, nor till he hears things, to be apprehensive. There is nothing more visible than what is secret, and nothing more manifest than what is minute. Therefore the superior man is watchful over himself, when he is alone. While there are no stirrings of pleasure, anger, sorrow, or joy, the mind may be said to be in the state of Equilibrium. When those feelings have been stirred, and they act in their due degree, there ensues what may be called the state of Harmony. This Equilibrium is the great root from which grow all the human actings in the world, and this Harmony is the universal path which they all should pursue.

The Mystic

Simone Weil
1909-1943

A conception of equilibrium

Equilibrium alone destroys and annuls force. Social order can be nothing but an equilibrium of forces. As it cannot be expected that a man without grace should be just, there must be a society organised in such a way that injustices punish each other through a perpetual oscillation. Equilibrium alone reduces force to nothing. If we know in what way society is unbalanced, we must do what we can to add weight to the lighter scale. Although the weight may consist of evil, in handling it with this intention, perhaps we do not become defiled. But we must have formed a conception of equilibrium and be ever ready to change sides like justice, 'that fugitive from the camp of conquerors'.

The Monk

Gautama Buddha
563–483BCE

The middle path

On one occasion the Blessed One ... addressed the group of five monks:
"Monks, these two extremes ought not to be practised by one who has gone forth from the household life. There is addiction to indulgence of sense-pleasures, which is low, coarse, the way of ordinary people, unworthy, and unprofitable; and there is addiction to self-mortification, which is painful, unworthy and unprofitable. Avoiding both these extremes, the The Perfect One has realised the Middle Path; it gives vision, gives knowledge, and leads to calm, to insight, to enlightenment and to Nirvana. And what is that Middle Path realised by the The Perfect One...? It is the Noble Eightfold path, and nothing else, namely: right understanding, right thought, right speech, right action, right livelihood, right effort, right mindfulness and right concentration. This is the Middle Path realised by the The Perfect One which gives vision, which gives knowledge, and leads to calm, to insight, to enlightenment, and to Nirvana."

Balance, equilibrium, equality, fairness –
individuals and societies have been striving for it
since first forming groups, and philosophers have
been grappling with it for almost as long. Here
are six thinkers' views on balance.

The Political Theorist

Hannah Arendt
1906–1975

A framework of stability

Man's urge for change and his need for stability have always balanced and checked each other, and our current vocabulary, which distinguishes between two factions, the progressives and the conservatives, indicates a state of affairs in which this balance has been thrown out of order. No civilisation – the man-made artefact to house successive generations – would ever have been possible without a framework of stability, to provide the wherein for the flux of change. Foremost among the stabilising factors, more enduring than customs, manners and traditions, are the legal systems that regulate our life in the world and our daily affairs with each other.

The Ethicist

Aristotle
384–322BCE

Deficiency and excess

First, then, we must consider this fact: that it is in the nature of moral qualities that they are destroyed by deficiency and excess, just as we can see (since we have to use the evidence of visible facts to throw light on those that are invisible) in the case of health and strength. For both excessive and insufficient exercise destroy one's strength, and both eating and drinking too much or too little destroy health, whereas the right quantity produces, increases and preserves it. So it is the same with temperance, courage and the other virtues. The man who shuns and fears everything and stands up to nothing becomes a coward; the man who is afraid of nothing at all, but marches up to every danger, becomes foolhardy. Similarly, the man who indulges in every pleasure and refrains from none becomes licentious; but if a man behaves like a boor and turns his back on every pleasure, he is a case of insensibility. Thus temperance and courage are destroyed by excess and deficiency and preserved by the mean.

The Materialist

Denis Diderot
1809–1882

The order of a moment

What is this world? A complex whole, subject to endless revolutions. All these revolutions show a continual tendency to destruction; a swift succession of beings who follow one another, press forward, and vanish; a fleeting symmetry; the order of a moment. I reproached you just now with estimating the perfection of things by your own capacity; and I might accuse you here of measuring its duration by the length of your own days. You judge of the continuous existence of the world, as an ephemeral insect might judge of yours. The world is eternal for you, as you are eternal to the being that lives but for one instant. Yet the insect is the more reasonable of the two. For what a prodigious succession of ephemeral generations attests your eternity! What an immeasurable tradition! Yet shall we all pass away, without the possibility of assigning either the real extension that we filled in space, or the precise time that we shall have endured. Time, matter, space – all, it may be, are no more than a point.

Walking the path

Interviewee: Michael Puett
Interview by Nigel Warburton

Nigel Warburton: From outside Chinese philosophy it seems that balance, and particularly within Daoism, is a crucial concept – it's the balance of forces, that's an idea that filters through to the West. Is that accurate, that balance does play a large part in Chinese philosophy?

Michael Puett: It does indeed. And one of the key reasons it's such a key part of Chinese philosophy is that one of the opening assumptions in China is: Imagine the world as a very messy world of constantly flowing energies, often very different energies and different modalities of energies. And therefore, in this world of constant energies things are endlessly bumping against each other, often in poor ways. And this is particularly bad

when you get to, for example, humans, who are also these messy things with tons of different energies going on, interplaying with other messy things with tons of energies (other human beings) and we tend to play off against each other very, very badly.

So, the background to a concern with balance is a sense that in a world where humans are interacting within it, is a world that's always in danger of conflict – where the messiness is always playing off with other messiness in bad ways, and if that's your opening concern then one of the things you want to do is to learn to work with these competing forces. You're not trying to even things out, you're not trying to marginalise things, you want to work with all of these different forces and connect them in ways that leads to some kind of flourishing. And there, and finally to get to the key term, the notion is that one of the goals you are seeking is to balance these different forces so no one of them is, for any lengthy amount of time, predominant over the others.

That's really interesting because one model of a balance is two pans with a pivot, and there are only two things to find a point of equilibrium between,

but the way you have described that, it sounds like there are many other aspects to this 'balance' thing.

Yes! Yes! Many. And this is one of the aspects that I think is often not well understood from the West, because it's understood – and this part is true – that two of the big divisions that energies can be categorised into is yin and yang. So think of yin as the female – "I'm cold" – yang is hot – male – and when we hear this we often think; "Oh, so that means there are two energies just as there are males and females, and the whole world is divided into two things", and therefore, as you said, it would simply be a question of balancing these two things. But of course, what's really important to Chinese philosophy is these categories go all the way down and are constantly intermixing.

So it's not that I, for example as a male, consist of yang energy, it's that I have a little bit more yang energy, which is why I'm male, but I have tons of yin energies – and it's energies in the plural – and moreover, these are interacting. I've got tons of these different energies in my body, some of which are yang and some of which are yin, these are interacting when I interact with other human beings I am interacting with their yang-ness and their yin-ness, and therefore it's not really two things that simply need to be balanced; you're really balancing a multiplicity of radically different forces.

So, to understand that, are you talking about these twin aspects of, for instance, anger or desire, what sort of things are they attached to?

Precisely. One of the things they can be attached to are what we would call emotions. So, if I get angry, in this way of thinking, what's happening is I'm getting an explosion of the yang form of energy. Which means, of course, if there's too much yang energy that we can call anger, I will become way overly aggressive, I will cease to see the complexities of situations because I will be overwhelmed with my aggressive angry energy, and therefore I need to balance it out with more moderate forms of energies. So, with my anger, I balance it out with more yin energy. And that's just internally, but of course if people are dealing with me in such a horrible state, what they would try to do is do things to bring about balancing – do things to calm down this overwhelming anger and do things to allow more of the yin energies to grow within me as well.

Now, people who are reading this won't be able to see your hands moving, but it's almost as if you were doing some kind of martial art when you were describing that. So the relations between people is about turning the energies into directions where it's being used in a positive way, much as a kind of, I don't know, whether in some kind of Kung Fu or whatever, you take the energy that somebody is using as they run towards you and turn it into a way of incapacitating them rather than getting a blow from them.

Precisely. So just as an example, in Judo, which means 'the way of softness' in Chinese, and the goal of this, and the key aspect of martial arts,

indeed you are trying to sense the energies of the other person and either work with those energies or use those energies against them if they are trying to attack you. So, in a prototypical example like the one you mentioned, if someone is aggressive towards me, they have an overreliance on a yang energy, by definition according to this way of thinking, that would lead them to be slightly overaggressive, slightly overreaching their resources. I'm trying to sense that moment and use the very energy they're using against me, against them. In a very literal sense in Judo, like someone trying to lunge at me, I simply shift my body within them and use that to throw them over me, for example.

So, I'm trying to understand the different aspects within which you're feeling this. So would it be possible, for instance, to be a balanced person, to have an overall equilibrium between these two forces, and yet in some respects, have an excess of one or the other? So in respect of, well we've talked about anger, but what about in terms of love – you have an excess of love – and I don't know which force of the two that would tend to be connected with – but then in some other aspect like anger you have a different balance, yet overall it all evens out. Is that a possibility? Or does each of the aspects in which yin and yang are visible or present, do they all have to be individually balanced in a kind of point of equilibrium, or are we looking at balance between the different aspects of the self?

Michael Puett, photo by Charles K. Michael

In a weird way, it's kind of both but adding in even a third element, which is: add in the temporal element. So, if the constant working of all energies in different situations in dealing with other people – who also have these very complex energies that are coming out, and so the sense would be no one of these energies – if it's preponderate for too long, will lead you in good directions; any of them. Because any of them, if they are completely preponderate will mean you will fail to see something else where it be overly focused on one thing and not on something else. So, you'd think, to give a standard example in the literature, well, being a warm-hearted person is of course a good thing. Well, the answer is 'usually', but if you're always being too warm there might be a moment when you're dealing with someone who you really need to be the stronger figure, for a brief moment. But obviously if you're too strong, that will work against that situation as well.

And so, the sense is in any situation you will have briefly the preponderance of one set of energies, but you're also becoming aware of the inherent dangers that will always set in when any set of energies are preponderant, and you're immediately trying to balance out. So, getting back to your question, at certain moments, yes, there will be a preponderance –

and that's even a good thing – but it's always dangerous if that continues for too long, pulling you into situations that would not be the appropriate set of energies for.

And is this philosophy of yin and yang exclusively attached to Daoism, or is it more general than that?

It's actually quite general. So it develops in a body of literature that's very much focused on these practices of working with your energies, and then the language is really taken over by both Daoism and Confucianism, and the reason is because regardless of your ultimate philosophical position on all sorts of issues concerning ethics, better ways to live, et cetera, it's an incredibly rich vocabulary to help the practitioner become incredibly self-conscious of sort of the complex, messy emotional dispositions that we all have, and with this terminology you have a very concrete way of learning to sense that, to work with that, to refine that, and so it really becomes an all-pervasive language across the different ways of thinking across China.

And is it the kind of language that you hear spoken – that somebody actually describes another person within that framework?

Oh, very much so, very much so. You can use it to describe people,

you can use it to describe foods – so sometimes if you're eating a meal it is slightly imbalanced. Not because, say, it's too spicy, but because it's too spicy and not being balanced off something else. And so, if you're serving one dish that has a high yang energy, you'll want to balance that with another dish that will moderate that a bit. And of course, again, you can think of this temporally – so at one moment in the meal I'll serve this really, really, really strong yang energy piece, and then balance this right afterwards with something much more moderate. And so, you can talk about people this way, you can talk about foods this way, you can talk about situations this way.

And I might add, along with yang and yin energies, another way to categorise them is in terms of levels of intensity. You can have high energy moments, low energy moments, high energy situations, low energy situations. You can have highly refined feelings of energy, you can have very poorly refined energy which means you're not highly responsive to situations. So, there are lots of different modalities you're learning to pay attention to that you're always trying to, in any given situation, balance out with the other ones.

So, is the energy different from the yin and yang, or is that a description of the yin and yang?

Instead of thinking, "I have some 'self' with some inherent set of personality that I should just accept," you're thinking, "No, I'm just a mess of different energy, as is everyone else and therefore I'm capable of becoming a more balanced human being."

Think of yin and yang as one possible way of categorising these different energies – so it's one very powerful way of categorising them, but you can also do categories on the level of refinement vs. lack of refinement. So, for example, air is highly, highly refined energy. Mud actually has some energy in it, but it's really, really, really low in terms of the refinement spectrum. And so the reason that way of thinking can be very helpful is we humans have some more highly refined energies within us and some very poorly refined energies and then the danger of the ways we live our lives is we can dissipate our higher energies, and the goal is to, on the contrary, develop practices that will allow us to, in a very literal sense, energise ourselves – so getting more high energy. So, if you're feeling very high energy from this way of thinking, you can practice and train yourself to be able to do that more commonly. But again, too much high energy in certain situations is a bad thing, which is why you need to balance it.

So, you spoke of air and mud. When I think of energy, I'm thinking of the things that allow me to feel strong and do things rather than being listless. And obviously breathing in air is a prerequisite of that, for everyone. Is that why air is high energy, or is it something independent of that, that it just is high energy because of some metaphysical assumptions that some Chinese philosophers make about air?

Well, partly it is. Part of the larger metaphysics would be: Think of the heavens above us as being extremely high energy. So, for example, if spirits exist up there, conceptualised as figures who are exceedingly high energy,

who can see perfectly, hear perfectly, interact and respond to other spirits and other natural forces perfectly, meaning that they are highly refined energy. Then below is the Earth. Say, again, we'll use our example of mud – very low refined energy, which means mud – it's not alive, it's not vital, it certainly cannot hear and listen. It does not react to anything, it can react to the pond, I can step on it and move it – but it can't respond. And air, getting back to your question, of course is more heavenly, mud is earthly.

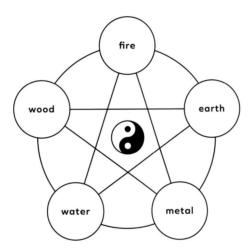

And the reason this matters so much to them is, of course, because humans are right in between. We have some life, so we have some vitality, we have some consciousness, we are capable of seeing and hearing, but we usually don't see terribly well – by which they mean seeing the world around us effectively. We don't really hear very well – we hear in limited perspectival ways – and so the goal of the self-cultivational gene is to train ourselves to become, well, more like those spirits above, right? More vital, more alive, able to see more clearly, hear more clearly, be more responsive

to the world around us. We're humans, so we'll never get there fully, but the goal is to become more like that in the ways we live our lives.

So do you think the way of seeing the world would be helpful to somebody who sees the world more scientifically, because in a sense, what's beneath the mud – maybe coal – could have high energy and what's above, as the air gets thinner, may be low energy in terms of what we can do with it to generate more power; though obviously the Sun has a lot of power. That's such a different way of conceptualising the world – is it useful to explore this, or should we treat it as an interesting feature of Chinese metaphysics to have divided up the world this way that somehow science has gotten beyond?

Yes. I think it's a very helpful way to think. And let me actually begin with humans, but then turn to the larger metaphysical world.

So, in terms of humans, very valuable. One of the dangers I think we fall into, particularly in the West and more recently, is we tend to fall into what from this perspective I would even call the 'danger' of thinking we have some pre-given authentic selves. So, I've got a self here, if I act in certain ways that's just me, that's just who I am, and I should be learning to love and embrace who I really am. Of course, from this perspective, you should never think that, because the current way you're feeling may simply be a set of energies playing out – and assume they're usually playing out pretty poorly – and then it's a question of developing practices to change it. So instead of thinking "I have some 'self' with some inherent set of personality traits that I should just accept", you're thinking, "No, I'm

Learn to train yourself to not be overly taken with emotional responses to the world that will lead you to be overly-aggressive, or even overly-happy.

just a mess of different energy, as is everyone else and therefore I'm capable of becoming a more balanced human being, as are those around me." I can work with others around me to create better situations. So, for humans, absolutely.

But let me also turn to your question about metaphysics here too. I think we tend to buy into similar notions when we read the larger cosmos. We tend to fall into, again from this perspective, a danger of reading the world of consisting of fundamental substances that just are what they are – that follow clear, natural, unchanging laws and if we can understand those laws, we can understand what the substances are and what the forces are that determine their interactions. Now, in certain ways of thinking this can be very productive, it leads to a reductive approach in the sciences that's been extraordinarily productive, there's

no question, but the danger of course is that it forces you to argue that the world really does consist of these fundamental substances with clearly definable, natural laws that govern their interaction, and I think it's worth posing the question that that's possibly just wrong. We certainly know at the quantum level that it's wrong; could it be wrong at a deeper level?

Imagine a world as we see very strongly worked out in Chinese metaphysics, that's always being thought of in these endless and ultimately not fully conceptualisable levels of interacting energies, and therefore you're not going to get clear natural laws that will define everything. You can talk in terms of patterns of interaction, but of course once you're using a term like 'patterns of interaction' you can ask: "Are the patterns always beneficial? Are there ways to work with these patterns in ways that would be more productive for us and other aspects of the larger natural world?" And once you're posing that question, as with humans, it allows you to then pose the questions of whether we could alter things that we otherwise accept as pre-given and unchangeable, and I think thinking that way can be extraordinarily productive.

You've talked about practices – and I know that Chinese philosophy is very much tied to developmental practices to change the way we think about things, particularly in the area of ethics – are there any specific practices tied to particular texts or schools that you think are important in achieving balance in individuals? I'm thinking of somebody reading this who wants to begin to explore Chinese philosophy. Are there pointers to texts and things to do which might jolt them into a different way of being in the world that is in better balance, in the way that you have been describing?

Absolutely. One text I would recommend in particular that does indeed

focus very much on practices, is a work called *The Inward Training*. It actually has a very good translation into English by Harold Roth, and the whole text is – it's one of the early texts, it's about the 4th century BCE – it is one of the early texts in China that really tries to work out the implications of thinking in terms of these modalities of different energies. The focus of the text is indeed the basic practices that we could begin engaging in, and the argument of the text is usually our daily practices consist of dissipating our *qi*, so dissipating our high level energies, and slowly over time we make ourselves tired and sick, bringing about a much earlier death than we would otherwise have to face. The key practice that the text wants to advocate are practices that teach us to, in a very literal since, live better and in an equally literal sense, become more energised. So it's all about – first some obvious things – learning to eat well and exercise…

We do say a 'balanced diet'!

Indeed, indeed! Absolutely crucial. But then it goes beyond that – the things we already accept – it goes beyond that and we'll say as well that equally, the ways we are emotionally involved in the world are also in danger and we need to learn to balance those. Learn to balance your interactions with those around you, learn to train yourself to not be overly taken with emotional responses to the world that will lead you to be overly-aggressive, or even overly-happy, which always will entail a fallback to sadness after the euphoria. And so you're training yourself to moderate and refine your responses to the world, which this text will say you should be doing right along with exercising, learning to eat well etc. It's part of the same regime of practices. And eating well and sleeping well we usually don't do, but we know we should – but this will say; well, equally think of this as a daily practice learning to work with your emotional dispositions, learning to work with your responses to the world. And once you begin thinking in terms of energies, it's very practical because you have a very concrete way to understand what they're talking about, because you can certainly feel these energies when you're practising. You can feel them when you exercise – you can equally feel them just when you're talking to people and working in situations.

That's brilliant. Is that text by a known author, and is it within a particular school of philosophy?

Intriguingly, no. Which goes back to your question about how pervasive these ideas are. This is one chapter in a miscellaneous text called the *Guanzi*, and Guanzi was just a major minister of one of the old states, the state of Qi, and this is simply a body of text that at least was claimed to have been written in this state. There's no author given to this particular chapter, simply known as *The Inward Training*. It's not classified according to any way of thinking; it simply presents itself as a teaching about energies. And yet once this and related texts are being written, this language just becomes pervasive in the tradition. And so then figures that we most certainly known very well – Mencius, Zheng Xuan – start picking up this language, but it seems to initially emerge out of a discussion of

self-cultivation and how to cultivate energies within the human body.

And is there a specific word for 'balance' that is used repeatedly, the thing that you're aiming for?

There is – the main term that's used is 'harmony'. And here too, harmony, when it's translated into English, it gives a slightly dangerous connotation, because we hear the word harmony and we think "Oh, that means it's all about harmonising things in the sense of homogenising things, making everything fit together." And in Chinese, the sense of harmony is, on the contrary, "No, no, no. Imagine a world of radically disparate, endlessly poorly-interacting energies, and harmony is not homogenising them, it's learning to connect them productively." And as you can see from that way of formulating it, what that will mean in any situation is going to be radically different, so you're learning to train yourself to sense these complexities, work with these complexities, connect these complexities. And that's what they really mean by harmony – you

don't get rid of the differences; you are actually working with the differences.

Well you could say that some kinds of harmony, in music, work with dissonances to resolve them eventually over time. So, there's a sense that Bach's harmonies have lots of dissonances, but they're resolved at the end of the piece usually, so the temporal element is absolutely crucial. The metaphor of balance is also important, but it's something else as well – it's almost like vectors, getting vectors to pull in the direction you want them to pull in rather than apart.

Yes, that's a very nice way of putting it. It would be, in a sense, going back to the music analogy, an endless work of these disparate notes that you're endlessly connecting without there ever being a final resolution because it's always going to be altering. And the moment you seem to get a perfect resolution, one moment later that's going to include something very dangerous that you hadn't noticed and will require some kind of new work of reweaving these different tonal patterns together. ◼

"This amazing app tells you when you are looking your phone too much!"

Empty space

Illustration by Aida Novoa & Carlos Egan

Thirty spokes unite at the single hub;
It is the empty space which makes the wheel useful.
Mould clay to form a bowl;
It is the empty space which makes the bowl useful.
Cut out windows and doors;
It is the empty space which makes the room useful.

By Laozi

From the *Tao Te Ching*, 6th
century BCE

Differences between man and woman

Simone de Beauvoir

by Simone de Beauvoir

Is it enough to change laws, institutions, customs, public opinion, and the whole social context, for men and women to become truly equal? "Women will always be women," say the sceptics. Other seers prophesy that in casting off their femininity they will not succeed in changing themselves into men and they will become monsters. This would be to admit that the woman of today is a creation of nature; it must be repeated once more that in human society nothing is natural and that woman, like much else, is a product elaborated by civilisation. The intervention of others in her destiny is fundamental: if this action took a different direction, it would produce a quite different result. Woman is determined not by her hormones or by mysterious instincts, but by the manner in which her body and her relation to the world are modified through the action of others than herself. The abyss that separates the adolescent boy and girl has been deliberately widened between them since earliest childhood; later on, woman could not be other than what she was made, and that past was bound to shadow her for life. If we appreciate its influence, we see clearly that her destiny is not predetermined for all eternity.

We must not believe, certainly, that a change in woman's economic condition alone is enough to transform her, though this factor has been and remains the basic factor in her evolution; but until it has brought about the moral, social, cultural, and other consequences that it promises and requires, the new woman cannot appear. At this moment they have been realised nowhere, in Russia no more than in France or the United States; and this explains why the woman of today is torn between the past and the future. She appears most often as a 'true woman' disguised as a man, and she feels herself as ill at ease in her flesh as in her masculine garb. She must shed her old skin and cut her own new clothes. This she could do only through a social evolution. No single educator could fashion a female human being today who would be the exact homologue of the male human being; if she is brought up like a boy, the young girl feels she is an oddity and thereby she is given a new kind of sex specification. Stendhal understood this when he said: "The forest must be planted all at once." But if we imagine, on the contrary, a society in which the equality of the sexes would be concretely realised, this equality would find new expression in each individual.

If the little girl were brought up from the first with the same demands and rewards, the same severity and the same freedom, as her brothers, taking part in the same studies, the same games, promised the same future, surrounded with women and men who seemed to her undoubted equals, the

meanings of the castration complex and of the Oedipus complex would be profoundly modified. Assuming on the same basis as the father the material and moral responsibility of the couple, the mother would enjoy the same lasting prestige; the child would perceive around her an androgynous world and not a masculine world. Were she emotionally more attracted to her father – which is not even sure – her love for him would be tinged with a will to emulation and not a feeling of powerlessness; she would not be oriented towards passivity. Authorised to test her powers in work and sports, competing actively with the boys, she would not find the absence of the penis – compensated by the promise of a child enough to give rise to an inferiority complex; correlatively the boy would not have a superiority complex if it were not instilled into him and if he looked up to women with as much respect as to men. [I knew a little boy of eight who lived with his mother, aunt and grandmother, all independent and active women, and his weak old half-crippled grandfather. He had a crushing inferiority complex in regard to the feminine sex, although he made efforts to combat it. At school he scorned comrades and teachers because they were miserable males.] The little girl would not seek sterile compensation in narcissism and dreaming, she would not take her fate for granted; she would be interested in what she was doing, she would throw herself without reserve into undertakings.
...

As a matter of fact, man, like woman, is flesh, therefore passive, the plaything of his hormones and of the species, the restless prey of his desires. And she, like him, in the midst of the carnal fever, is a consenting, a voluntary gift, an activity; they live out in their several fashions the strange ambiguity of existence made body. In those combats where they think

they confront one another, it is really against the self that each one struggles, projecting into the partner that part of the self which is repudiated; instead of living out the ambiguities of their situation, each tries to make the other bear the objection and tries to reserve the honour for the self. If, however, both should assume the ambiguity with a clear-sighted modesty, correlative of an authentic pride, they would see each other as equals and would live out their erotic drama in amity. The fact that we are human beings is infinitely more important than all the peculiarities that distinguish human beings from one another; it is never the given that confers superiorities: "virtue", as the ancients called it, is defined at the level of "that which depends on us". In both sexes is played out the same drama of the flesh and the spirit, of finitude and transcendence; both are gnawed away by time and laid in wait for by death, they have the same essential need for one another; and they can gain from their liberty the same glory. If they were to taste it, they would no longer be tempted to dispute fallacious privileges, and fraternity between them could then come into existence.

I shall be told that all this is utopian fancy, because woman cannot be transformed unless society has first made her really the equal of man. Conservatives have never failed in such circumstances to refer to that vicious circle; history, however, does not revolve. If a caste is kept in a state of inferiority, no doubt it remains inferior; but liberty can break the circle. Let the Negroes vote and they become worthy of having the vote; let woman be given responsibilities and she is able to assume them. The fact is that oppressors cannot be expected to make a move of gratuitous generosity; but at one time the revolt of the oppressed, at another time even the very evolution of the privileged caste

The fact that we are human beings is infinitely more important than all the peculiarities that distinguish human beings from one another.

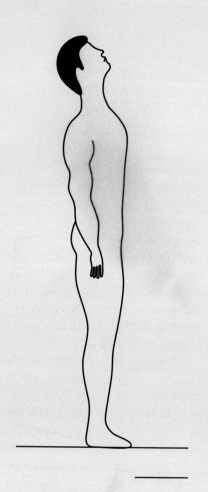

Photo: Simone de Beauvoir and Jean-Paul Sartre

itself, creates new situations; thus men have been led, in their own interest, to give partial emancipation to women: it remains only for women to continue their ascent, and the successes they are obtaining are an encouragement for them to do so. It seems almost certain that sooner or later they will arrive at complete economic and social equality, which will bring about an inner metamorphosis.

However this may be, there will be some to object that if such a world is possible it is not desirable. When woman is 'the same' as her male, life will lose its salt and spice. This argument, also, has lost its novelty: those interested in perpetuating present conditions are always in tears about the marvellous past that is about to disappear, without having so much as a smile for the young future. It is quite true that doing away with the slave trade meant death to the great plantations, magnificent

with azaleas and camellias, it meant ruin to the whole refined Southern civilisation. In the attics of time rare old laces have joined the clear pure voices of the *Sistine castrati*, and there is a certain 'feminine charm' that is also on the way to the same dusty repository. I agree that he would be a barbarian indeed who failed to appreciate exquisite flowers, rare lace, the crystal-clear voice of the eunuch, and feminine charm.

When the 'charming woman' shows herself in all her splendour, she is a much more exalting object than the 'idiotic paintings, over-doors, scenery, showman's garish signs, popular reproductions', that excited Rimbaud; adorned with the most modern artifices, beautified according to the newest techniques, she comes down from the remoteness of the ages, from Thebes, from Crete, from Chichén-Itzá; and she is also the totem set up

deep in the African jungle; she is a helicopter and she is a bird; and there is this, the greatest wonder of all: under her tinted hair the forest murmur becomes a thought, and words issue from her breasts. Men stretch forth avid hands towards the marvel, but when they grasp it it is gone; the wife, the mistress, speak like everybody else through their mouths: their words are worth just what they are worth; their breasts also. Does such a fugitive miracle – and one so rare – justify us in perpetuating a situation that is baneful for both sexes? One can appreciate the beauty of flowers, the charm of women, and appreciate them at their true value; if these treasures cost blood or misery, they must be sacrificed.

But in truth this sacrifice seems to men a peculiarly heavy one; few of them really wish in their hearts for woman to succeed in making it; those among them who hold woman in contempt see in the sacrifice nothing for them to gain, those who cherish her see too much that they would lose. And it is true that the evolution now in progress threatens more than feminine charm alone: in beginning to exist for herself, woman will relinquish the function as double and mediator to which she owes her privileged place in the masculine universe; to man, caught between the silence of nature and the demanding presence of other free beings, a creature who is at once his like and a passive thing seems a great treasure. The guise in which he conceives his companion may be mythical, but the experiences for which she is the source or the pretext are none the less real: there are hardly any more precious, more intimate, more ardent. There is no denying that feminine dependence, inferiority, woe, give women their special character; assuredly woman's autonomy, if it spares men many troubles, will also deny them many conveniences; assuredly there are certain forms of the sexual adventure which will be lost in the world of tomorrow. But this does not mean that love, happiness, poetry, dream, will be banished from it.

Let us not forget that our lack of imagination always depopulates the future; for us it is only an abstraction; each one of us secretly deplores the absence there of the one who was himself. But the humanity of tomorrow will be living in its flesh and in its conscious liberty; that time will be its present and it will in turn prefer it. New relations of flesh and sentiment of which we have no conception will arise between the sexes; already, indeed, there have appeared between men and women friendships, rivalries, complicities, comradeships – chaste or sensual – which past centuries could not have conceived. To mention one point, nothing could seem more debatable than the opinion that dooms the new world to uniformity and hence to boredom. I fail to see that this present world is free from boredom or that liberty ever creates uniformity.

To begin with, there will always be certain differences between man and woman; her eroticism, and therefore her sexual world, have a special form of their own and therefore cannot fail to engender a sensuality, a sensitivity, of a special nature. This means that her relations to her own body, to that of the male, to the child, will never be identical with those the male bears to his own body, to that of the female, and to the child; those who make much of 'equality in difference' could not with good grace refuse to grant me the possible existence of differences in equality. Then again, it

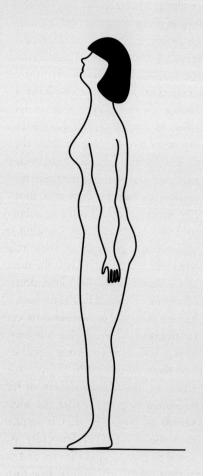

Those who make much of 'equality in difference' could not with good grace refuse to grant me the possible existence of differences in equality.

is institutions that create uniformity. Young and pretty, the slaves of the harem are always the same in the sultan's embrace; Christianity gave eroticism its savour of sin and legend when it endowed the human female with a soul; if society restores her sovereign individuality to woman, it will not thereby destroy the power of love's embrace to move the heart.

It is nonsense to assert that revelry, vice, ecstasy, passion, would become impossible if man and woman were equal in concrete matters; the contradictions that put the flesh in opposition to the spirit, the instant to time, the swoon of immanence to the challenge of transcendence, the absolute of pleasure to the nothingness of forgetting, will never be resolved; in sexuality will always be materialised the tension, the anguish, the joy, the frustration, and the triumph of existence. To emancipate woman is to refuse to confine her to the relations she bears to man, not to deny them to her; let her have her independent existence and she will continue none the less to exist for him also: mutually recognising each other as subject, each will yet remain for the other an other. The reciprocity of their relations will not do away with the miracles – desire, possession, love, dream, adventure – worked by the division of human beings into two separate categories; and the words that move us – giving, conquering, uniting – will not lose their meaning. On the contrary, when we abolish the slavery of half of humanity, together with the whole system of hypocrisy that it implies, then the 'division' of humanity will reveal its genuine significance and the human couple will find its true form. "The direct, natural, necessary relation of human creatures is the relation of man to woman," Marx has said. "The nature of this relation determines to what point man himself is to be considered as a generic being, as mankind; the relation of man to woman is the most natural relation of human being to human being. By it is shown, therefore, to what point the natural behaviour of man has become human or to what point the human being has become his natural being, to what point his human nature has become his nature."

The case could not be better stated. It is for man to establish the reign of liberty in the midst of the world of the given. To gain the supreme victory, it is necessary, for one thing, that by and through their natural differentiation men and women unequivocally affirm their brotherhood. ◼

Extract from *The Second Sex*, 1949.

"Glass ceiling? Looks like a glass floor to me."

NewPhilosopher

Back issues

Missed out on some of the previous editions? Well, you can now purchase copies for delivery worldwide, with prompt shipment from our UK and Australian warehouses.
Order now at www.newphilosopher.com/shop

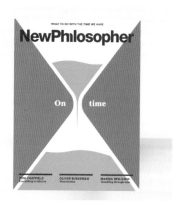

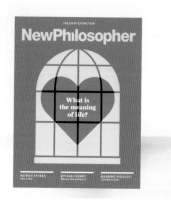

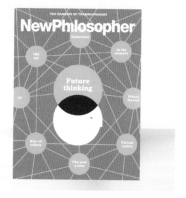

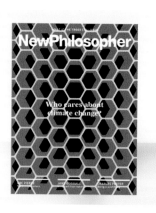

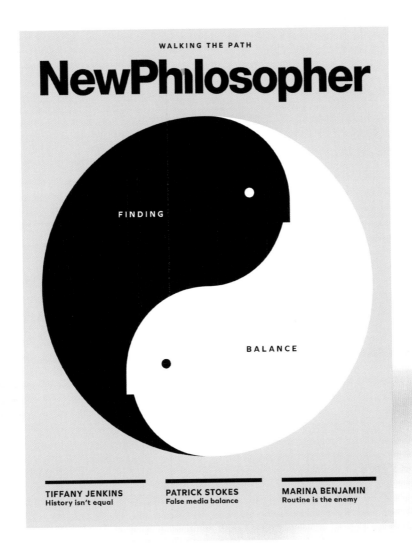

Choose a subscription

1 year	2 years	3 years
$60 AU/US	$115 AU/US	$150 AU/US
€39 UK	€75 UK	€110 UK
€55 EU/CAN	€105 EU/CAN	€140 EU/CAN
€65 Rest of the world	€125 Rest of the world	€159 Rest of the world

Digital subscriptions available from $30 for one year.
Digital + print subscriptions from $80 for 1 year.

www.newphilosopher.com/subscribe
Support New Philosopher magazine by taking out a subscription today.

newphilosopher.com

New Philosopher is located at 130 Macquarie Street, Hobart Tasmania 7000, Australia.
We offer delivery worldwide from our UK and Australian warehouses.

Here we present the winners of *New Philosopher* Writers' Award XXII: time. In first place is writer Ian Rose for his piece "Backwards in time". Professor of philosophy Barbara Ellen Hannan has taken out second place for her essay "The self in time".

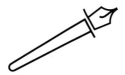

Backwards in time

by Ian Rose

It's precisely at this moment, again and again, that I'm catapulted backwards in time.

As the preamble ends (in this episode, the shop assistant, working late and alone, pulls back the curtain on the change cubicle, having received no response to her "are you alright in there?" only to reveal the looming, unmistakeable metallic form of, yes, a *cyberman*) and the opening titles and theme tune kick in, it feels as though the decades contract.

When that 1950s era blue Police Box begins its rotation through the vortex, propulsive bass, four-four tempo, and squalling synth underscoring its apparently eternal passage, I might as well be eight years old again, as sitting here, close to fifty, flanked by my

own children, seven and nine, watching *Doctor Who*.

Parenthood elasticates time.

During the early years of sleep upheaval and nappy-changing, vomity-shouldered, toy-strewn drudgery, every day seems to stretch beyond endurance, while the years flash by like comets. This effect is reinforced with school, the inarguable progress through grades, the tyranny of timetables and extra-curricular schedules, birthday cakes and holidays, the unforgiving pencil marks on the door frame that document the growth of our offspring, their subtext our own march toward oblivion.

Take heart, wrote (writes? will write and forever be writing?) Einstein in his letter to the grieving fam-

ily of recently-parted buddy, Michele Besso, for "the distinction between past, present and future is only a stubbornly persistent illusion".

I came to fatherhood late, by accident rather than design, but was gratified by the inadvertent neatness of the timing. My fortieth birthday came one month before our first-born, which besides making it easy to remember my age and hers, also provides a clear and emboldened line to separate the before and after. Because we do love to compartmentalise experience, both the collective and personal kind, to sort time, illusory though it may be, into *eras*.

And, just as everyone warned and promised, this really was the dawning of a new one. Life changed with

WINNER

WRITERS' AWARD XXII:
TIME

parenthood, utterly and irreversibly. I was braced for the terrifying boundlessness of unconditional love, and having to listen to *The Wiggles*. What I wasn't prepared for was how this new state would reconnect me with my own distant boyhood.

Seeing the world through our baby's eyes, I remembered the texture of the rough green fabric on the sofa towards which I'd crawled (am crawling, always will be), in a West London council flat, half a world and several decades away. The unhappy grind of teething on a rusk.

Through countless moments – watching them at play, catching my mother's old maxims on my lips, sitting through a school assembly – I am broadsided by the past's immediacy; its *presence*.

Looking in on the kids, an hour or so after settling them in their beds, and seeing through their scrunch-lidded sleep-pretence, I recollect lying awake at their age, tuned in to the murmur of grown-up conversation, the gurgle of glasses filling (it was the seventies, there was much gurgling), the theme-tunes of forbidden post-watershed television shows – the mischievous *Monty Python*, the thrilling *Hawaii Five-O*.

And now this, our *Doctor Who* communion.

For those in the dark, the titular Doctor is a time and space-travelling alien (a Time Lord from the planet Gallifrey) who careens around the universe in a police telephone-box ("But… it's bigger on the inside!" marvels just about every one of the human companions he/she's picked up along the way since the show's inception in 1963). He/she is over 900 years old and free from the strictures of mortality, the ageing process and, more recently, gender, 'regenerating' each time the principal actor tires of the role or proves a flop.

The Doctor's central tragedy is that she/he strives (always has strived, and ever will) to do good, to save and elevate living creatures everywhere, yet leaves a trail of ruined lives and death in his/her labyrinthine, space-time wake.

I adored the character and series as a child, though it was more about the monsters than all the ethical dilemmas and paradoxes. And now our kids are infatuated, too – not my doing, accidental and somewhat solipsistic a parent though I may be.

And these weekly sessions we share, catching up on the last several years' seasons (they've already witnessed three regenerations – I think our son enjoys these even more than the grotesquery, and regularly play-acts his own mutations, stiff as a board, in crucifixion pose, emitting a raspy growl that sounds a bit like a washing-machine limbering up for its spin cycle) are an unexpected treat, and a reminder of the mysterious nature of what the Doctor calls "wibbly, wobbly, timey-wimey".

Of course, you needn't be a Doctor Who fan or parent to intuit the wibbly-wobbliness of time.

Like so much else, the Greeks were on to it. It's right there in the language they used to differentiate our experience of time – *kronos* for the linear procession of minutes into hours, weeks into months and years, the stuff that nowadays has us stressing out, chasing deadlines, lamenting that our days don't contain enough of it; and *kairos*, which in classical rhetoric denotes the opportune moment (the term may stem from archery, and the perfect instant to release an arrow from its bow – time-conceits and arrows have correlated through the ages), but more generally describes those ineffable and extraordinary moments and occasions that seem to sidestep *kronos*'s (or chronological) parameters.

Even a human who doesn't choose to ponder this kind of thing, and abhors sci-fi in any form, understands that time flies when they're having fun, and a watched pot never boils. The metaphysics of time may boggle the mind, but they're also (and *at the same time*) common sense.

Another common experience for, in particular, the ageing human (and,

WINNER

WRITERS' AWARD XXII: TIME

facing down my half-century, I am forced, in spite of ongoing and determined denial, to count myself one) is the retention of childhood memories with greater acuity than the more recent. Casual research has confirmed I'm not alone in being able to recall the names, faces, and foibles of my primary school classmates more keenly than those of people I've met or worked with over the past few years, or even months, to my regular embarrassment.

And perhaps this stems from what Rousseau described as the childish brain's "suppleness that renders him suited for receiving all sorts of impressions". That trailblazer of the Enlightenment found children to hold little in the way of semantic memory (and thus most conventional education futile), but recognised that the adult memory will be drawn to childhood

as to a magnet, due to the enduring intensity of those impressions.

Sitting here, squeezed between my cooing kids, as we watch the 11th Doctor battle the cybermen, I am unable to summon the plot details of the 4th doing the same back in the seventies. But I remember how it *felt* to be huddled with my sister on that lumpy green sofa, faces hidden behind cushions in blissful dread.

Our mother's voice from the kitchen, telling us tea is ready. And, yes, Einstein's notion that she calls us yet and always will is a consolation, but not enough, not nearly enough.

She died, our mum, and so will I (am already dying, and always have been), both far earlier than I'd prefer. My only regeneration will spring from the memories these children hold of moments like this, though I remind

myself, every day, how lucky I am to have that, at least.

It may be wibbly wobbly, this timey-wimey, but our own is cruelly finite, and relentless in its passing.

Not one of us wastes it, in reflecting on this truth from time to time.

It might be nice to be like the Doctor: a Time Lord. It's easy to feel, though, that far from its lords, we are just serfs of the clock, the schedule, the calendar, the deepening lines on our faces describing our bondage to time. But it doesn't have to be that way. We can free ourselves from the shackles.

Liberation from the *kronos* comes from understanding and celebration of the *kairos*. Our finest guides through this deliverance, with their unthinking and enlightened immersion in the moment, must surely be children.

Whether our own, or our selves. ◘

Photo: Davros, Doctor Who Experience

RUNNER-UP

The self in time

by Barbara Ellen Hannan

When I tell people that I am a professor of philosophy, and that I do metaphysics, I am usually greeted with either blank stares or scepticism. When the person I am talking with is a scientist, I get even worse than scepticism: I get raised eyebrows and the instant conclusion that am I a goofy flake, not an intelligent person, not an educated person, and that there is no need to talk with me any further.

This dismissive attitude of scientists toward metaphysics is the unfortunate legacy of a misguided philosophy of science called 'logical positivism', or 'logical empiricism', that was influential during most of the 20th century. According to logical positivism, only science is meaningful; metaphysics is nonsense. The logical positivists thought there was a way to distinguish clearly between science and metaphysics. They were wrong about that. They were wrong in just about everything they preached, as it turns out. But there are still a lot of people around who think metaphysics is nonsense, without being able to say clearly what metaphysics is or why they think it is nonsense. (Sigh.)

Metaphysical problems are quite real, and scientists are (or at least ought to be) interested in them.

A good definition of a metaphysical problem in the modern sense comes from Wilfrid Sellars: a clash between "the manifest image" and "the scientific image".

As practical, active human beings living our lives, we must assume certain things to be true. For example: we are rational agents, with beliefs and desires, goals and interests, and free will; we can make choices and perform voluntary acts that have effects on the future; the past is over and gone, and the future is not yet; and so forth. This kind of thing is what Sellars called the manifest image – the way we and our world seem, to common sense and practical reason, to be.

As human beings living in the scientific age, we are constantly challenged to adjust our manifest image of reality so that it coheres with the way *science* tells us things are – the sci-

entific image. When there is a clash between the manifest image and the scientific image, and we cannot seem to let go of the manifest image and accept what science says, we have a metaphysical problem.

I would add the following to what Sellars said: another kind of metaphysical problem arises when the scientific image contradicts itself, or seems to defy reason. A good example is the apparent ability of a quantum of energy to be in a superposition of states, simultaneously headed toward slit A and headed toward slit B. (Can this be so? Can a cat be both alive and dead at the same time?)

The scientific image of the self

According to science, persons are (or, more accurately, are constituted by) biological organisms.

An organism is a space-time 'worm', an entity extended in the three familiar spatial dimensions, and also in the fourth dimension, time.

The space-time worm that constitutes me begins in the late 1950s, and

RUNNER-UP

WRITERS' AWARD XXII: TIME

Photo: Dworcowy clock, Wroclaw

ends when I die, whenever that is.

An organism is a complex physical structure. There is no immaterial mind or soul; to speak of the soul is a misleading way of speaking of some of the life-functions of the organism, including the capacities for consciousness and voluntary action.

The self is not reliably a unified, coherent subject of perception and performer of rational action. The unity and rationality of the human subject are fragile and precarious. The brain possesses numerous systems and sub-systems which can be in conflict with each other, and only some of these systems are accessible to consciousness.

The scientific image of time

Einstein's theory of general relativity encourages us to think of time as the fourth dimension in which we exist, analogous in many ways to the spatial dimensions (up/down; right/left; forward/backward). We live in a space-time 'block universe': past, present, and future are equally real. Events can be located by reference to a set of coordinates both spatial and temporal. Time does not really 'flow' or 'pass' – the passage of time is a mere appearance.

Einstein's theory of special relativity, by contrast, tells us that time does pass, but it passes more slowly in a reference frame accelerating rapidly with respect to the observer (or, equivalently, in an increasingly strong gravitational field). There is no fact of the matter as

to whether two events are simultaneous; it depends on who is moving with respect to whom.

So, does time really pass or not? Physics itself appears undecided. This is the second kind of metaphysical problem defined above, a conflict within science itself.

[At least one philosopher, Donald C. Williams, argued that time does not really pass (flow or move). His argument was purely logical: motion can be defined only by reference to time: to move is to be in different places at different times. So, if time itself moved, it would have to move by reference to something else – (meta-time?). But meta-time would itself have to move, and this would require meta-meta-time. This line of thought leads to an unacceptable infinite regress. So, time does not move.]

The manifest image of the self

If I am a space-time 'worm', I do not experience myself as such. I experience myself only as, so to speak, the current time-slice. To myself, I seem to be an ego, a unified point of view, a subject of perception and thought, sliding along the space-time worm, *real* only in the ephemeral present instant. I can access past time-slices of myself only by means of that fallible faculty: memory. I can access future time-slices of myself only by means of that even more fallible faculty: anticipation. My past selves do not seem real to me – they are gone, in the past, and the past is over. My future selves, it seems, are not yet real. They are in the future, and the future is not yet.

Time surely *seems* to move or flow. We have many metaphors capturing the intuition of time's passage: time

RUNNER-UP

WRITERS' AWARD XXII:
TIME

---

marches on; time waits for no man; time is a river. "So we beat on, boats against the current, borne back ceaselessly into the past," wrote F. Scott Fitzgerald in *The Great Gatsby*, and so it seems. Events are in the future; then, for a fleeting instant, they are present; and then they recede ever more distantly into the past.

There are some counter-intuitive consequences of the scientific hypothesis that I am (or am constituted by) a space-time worm. Consider *change*. If I am a space-time worm, then I change over time only in the sense that different temporal segments or slices of me have different properties, entirely analogous to the spatial situation of a road that is bumpy in some places, smooth in others, curved in some places, straight in others, and so on. But this seems wrong. Change is a dynamic process. Time-slices seem like fictions, freeze-frames taken from a continuous flow.

If time-slices were real, it seems we ought to be able to count them. We ought to possess some clear criterion establishing where one ends and another begins. W.V.O. Quine refused to admit any entity into his ontology if it failed this test. "No entity without identity," he said, meaning that we should not admit any type of thing as real unless we can specify when we have one such thing, and when we have more than one. Time-slices fail Quine's test. How many time-slices constitute me?

How thin can you slice a space-time worm? It seems, upon reflection, that a space-time worm has an infinite number of slices, much as a line has an infinite number of points on it, or a measure of music has an infinite number of beats in it. (A piece marked with the meter signature 6/8 could equally well be marked 12/16, or 24/32... and you could go on doubling the fraction infinitely.)

When a banana changes from green to yellow to black, or when I change from young to middle-aged to old, the process is gradual and continual. There is *not* just a static space-time object, consisting of a countable number of temporal slices that have different properties. Rather, the properties of the thing change as time passes. The process is real, and the slices are fictions... or so it seems to me.

Another counter-intuitive consequence of the space-time worm theory of the self is that I am never wholly present at any given time. My friends never see all of me, even if they walk around me in a circle and survey my body from all sides. All they ever see is some time-segment of me.

Furthermore, according to the space-time worm theory, when I remember something that happened to me in the past, this indicates only that some time-segment of me, causally continuous with current time-segments of me, overlapped with the relevant past event. But this seems wrong, too. If I remember something that

happened to me when I was twenty years old, this is in virtue of the fact that *I was there* – I, the very same ego now typing this sentence, experienced the past event. I was wholly present then, and I am wholly present now.

Could the feeling that time moves be an illusion? Not, it seems to me, unless causation is also an illusion (and what could be more essential to science than causality?) Causation (which is essential to change) is a process in time, with a definite temporal order. Putting aside cases in which cause and effect are arguably simultaneous (such as a moving belt turning a pulley), causes usually precede their effects in time. The very existence of real causal relations among things presupposes that time has a direction ('time's arrow'). Physicists tell us that the direction of time is the direction of entropy, from order to disorder. But if time has a direction, then time moves.

I could say a lot more about the counter-intuitive consequences of the scientific image of time. For instance, if the 'block universe' is actual, then fatalism must be true: sentences about the future already have truth-values, and there is nothing we can do to alter the future. As practical agents, we simply cannot live as if fatalism were true.

Reflection on time and the self reveals that metaphysics, far from being nonsense, is continuous with science. Scientists still deluded by the legacy of logical positivism need to think again. ◼

Writers' award

Word length up to 1500 words, the winner receives $1000 and will have their work published in the next edition of New Philosopher magazine.

Award XXIII being human.
Closes 31 May 2019

Award XXIV balance.
Closes 31 August 2019

Email your piece to
ab@newphilosopher.com

For full details visit
www.newphilosopher.com/articles/prize
Open to subscribers only.

NewPhilosopher

womankind

Brought to you by the *New Philosopher* team, *Womankind* magazine is available in bookstores and newsstands in Australia, NZ, the US, Canada, the EU, and the UK.

Our library

The Cyber Effect

Mary Aiken
Shut-up toys

Somewhere along the line, a misinterpretation of neuroscience has led parents to believe that all stimulation for a child is good stimulation. They believe, wrongly, that a young brain must be kept constantly challenged and engaged. It's as if parents fear their toddler will become bored with real life, which I guess means life without a screen. And fearing a toddler tantrum may be another reason that tablets and mobile phones are pulled out of handbags and totes by parents and caregivers to placate and pacify young children. I have seen articles by psychologists referring to these as "shut-up toys".

The Path

Michael Puett & Christine Gross-Loh
Patterns of behaviour

Many of the Chinese thinkers would argue that you are not and should not think of yourself as a single, unified being. Let's say that you think of yourself as someone with a temper; someone who gets angry easily. The thinkers we are about to encounter would argue that you should not say, "Well, that's just the way I am," and embrace yourself for who you are. As we will see, perhaps you aren't inherently an angry person. Perhaps you simply slipped into ruts – patterns of behaviour – that you allowed to define who you thought you were. The truth is that you have just as much potential to be, say, gentle or forgiving as you do to be angry.

A Woman Looking At Men Looking At Women

Siri Hustvedt
Locus of identity

The face is the locus of identity – the place on the body to which we give our attention. We do not recognise people by their hands and feet, even those intimate to us. Infants only hours old can imitate the facial expressions of adults, although they do not know what or whom they are looking at and will not be able to recognise their own images in the mirror for many months to come. Babies seem to have a visual-moto-sensory awareness of the other person's face, what some researchers have called a "like-me" response that results in imitation, also referred to as "primary intersubjectivity".

Food for thought from the *New Philosopher* library. We discover books that can change the way you view the world.

The Case For Working With Your Hands

The Narcissism Epidemic

Walden; or, Life in the Woods

Matthew Crawford

Habits of mind

Mechanical work has required me to cultivate different intellectual habits. Further, habits of mind have an ethical dimension that we don't often think about. Good diagnosis requires attentiveness to the machine, almost a conversation with it, rather than assertiveness, as in the position papers produced on K Street. Cognitive psychologists speak of "metacognition", which is the activity of stepping back and thinking about your own thinking. It is what you do when you stop for a moment in your pursuit of a solution, and wonder whether your understanding of the problem is adequate.

Jean Twenge

The starter market

Sweet & Sassy, a Texas-based salon for girls, offers a package in which the girl is picked up at her door by a pink limo. Some girls go to adult salons and have manicures and pedicures – at age 7, sometimes as a birthday party event. First- through third-graders are also wearing makeup more often: in a 2007 survey, 55 per cent of 6- to 9-year-old girls said they used lip gloss or lipstick, and 65 per cent said they used nail polish. Cosmetics companies now refer to this age group as "the starter market." "We live in a culture of insta-celebrity," said marketing executive Samantha Skey. "Our little girls now grow up thinking they need to be ready for their close-up, lest the paparazzi arrive."

Henry David Thoreau

Equilibrium of nature

In April the pigeons were seen again flying express in small flocks, and in due time I heard the martins twittering over my clearing, though it had not seemed that the township contained so many that it could afford me any, and I fancied that they were peculiarly of the ancient race that dwelt in hollow trees ere white men came. In almost all climes the tortoise and the frog are among the precursors and heralds of this season, and birds fly with song and glancing plumage, and plants spring and bloom, and winds blow, to correct this slight oscillation of the poles and preserve the equilibrium of nature.

On Tolerance

By Zhūangzi

There has been such a thing as letting mankind alone and tolerance; there has never been such a thing as governing mankind. Letting alone Springs from the fear lest men's natural dispositions be perverted and tolerance springs from the fear lest their character be corrupted. But if their natural dispositions be not perverted, nor their character corrupted, what need is there left for government?

Of old, when Yao governed the empire, he made the people live happily; consequently, the people struggled to be happy and became restless. When Chieh governed the empire, he made the people live miserably; consequently the people regarded life as a burden and were discontented. Restlessness and discontent are subversive of virtue; and without virtue there has never been such a thing as stability.

When man rejoices greatly, he gravitates towards yang (the positive pole). When he is in great anger, he gravitates towards yin (the negative pole). If the equilibrium of positive and negative is disturbed, the four seasons are upset, and the balance of heat and cold is destroyed, man himself suffers physically thereby. It causes men to rejoice and sorrow inordinately, to live disorderly lives, to be vexed in their thoughts, and to lose their balance and form of conduct. When that happens, then

the whole world seethes with revolt and discontent, and we have such men as Robber Cheh, Tseng, and Shih. Offer the entire world as rewards for the good or threaten the wicked with the dire punishments of the entire world, and it is still insufficient (to reform them). Consequently, with the entire world, one cannot furnish sufficient inducements or deterrents to action. From the Three Dynasties downwards, the world has lived in a helter-skelter of promotions and punishments. What chance have the people left for living the even tenor of their lives?

Besides, love (over-refinement) of vision leads to debauchery in colour; love of hearing leads to debauchery in sound; love of charity leads to confusion in virtue; love of duty leads to perversion of principles; love of ceremonies (li) leads to a common fashion for technical skill; love of music leads to common lewdness of thought; love of wisdom leads to a fashion for the arts; and love of knowledge leads to a fashion for criticism If the people are allowed to live out the even tenor of their lives, the above eight may or may not be; it matters not. But if the people are not allowed to live out the even tenor of their lives, then these eight cause discontent and contention and strife, and throw the world into chaos.

Yet the world worships and cherishes them. Indeed, deep-seated is the mental chaos of the world. Is it merely a passing mistake that can be simply removed? Yet they observe fasts before their discussion, bend down on their knees to practise them, and sing and beat the drum and dance to celebrate them. What can I do about it?

Therefore, when a gentleman is unavoidably compelled to take charge of the government of the empire, there is nothing better than inaction (letting alone). By means of inaction only can he allow the people to live out the even tenor of their lives. Therefore, he who values the world as his own self may then be entrusted with the government of the world and he who loves the world as his own self may then be entrusted with the care of the world. Therefore if the gentleman can refrain from disturbing the internal economy of man, and from glorifying the powers of sight and hearing, he can sit still like a corpse or spring into action like a dragon, be silent as the deep or talk with the voice of thunder, the movements of his spirit calling forth the natural mechanism of Heaven. He can remain calm and leisurely doing nothing, while all things are brought to maturity and thrive. What need then would have I to set about governing the world?

Ts'ui Chu: asked Lao Tan, saying, "If the empire is not to be governed, how are men's hearts to be kept good?"

"Be careful," replied Lao Tan, "not to interfere with the natural goodness of the heart of man. Man's heart may be forced down or stirred up. In each case the issue is fatal. By gentleness, the hardest heart may be softened. But try to cut and polish it, and it will glow like fire or freeze like ice. In the twinkling of an eye it will pass beyond the limits of the Four Seas. In repose, it is profoundly still; in motion, it flies up to the sky. Like an unruly horse, it cannot be held in check. Such is the human heart."

Of old, the Yellow Emperor first interfered with the natural goodness of the heart of man, by means of charity and duty. In consequence, Yao and Shun wore the hair off their legs and the flesh off their arms in endeavouring to feed their people's bodies. They tortured the people's internal economy in order to conform to charity and duty. They exhausted the people's energies to live in accordance with the laws and statutes. Even then they did not succeed. Thereupon, Yao had to confine Huantou on Mount Ts'ung, exile the chiefs of the Three Miaos and their people into the Three Weis, and banish the Minister of Works to Yutu, which shows he had not succeeded. When it came to the times of the Three Kings, the empire was in a state of foment. Among the bad men were Chieh and Cheh; among the good were Tseng and Shih. By and by, the Confucianists and the Motseanists arose; and then came confusion between joy and anger, fraud between the simple and the cunning, recrimination between the virtuous and the evil-minded, slander between the honest and the liars, and the world order collapsed. Then the great virtue lost its unity, men's lives were frustrated. When there was a general rush for knowledge, the people's desires ever went beyond their possessions. The next thing was then to invent axes and saws, to kill by laws and statutes, to disfigure by chisels and awls. The empire seethed with discontent, the blame for which rests upon those who would interfere with the natural goodness of the heart of man.

In consequence, virtuous men sought refuge in mountain caves, while rulers of great states sat trembling in their ancestral halls. Then, when dead men lay about pillowed on each other's corpses, when cangued prisoners jostled each other in crowds and condemned criminals were seen everywhere, then the Confucianists and the Motseanists bustled about and rolled up their sleeves in the midst of gyves and fetters! Alas, they know not shame, nor what it is to blush!

Until I can say that the wisdom of Sages is not a fastener of cangues, and that charity of heart and duty to one's neighbour are not bolts for gyves, how should I know that Tseng and Shih were not the singing arrows (forerunners) of (the gangsters) Chieh and Cheh? Therefore it is said, "Abandon wisdom and discard knowledge, and the empire will be at peace."

The Yellow Emperor sat on the throne for nineteen years, and his laws obtained all over the empire. Hearing that Kuangch'engtse was living on Mount K'ungt'ung, he went there to see him, and said, "I am told that you are in possession of perfect Tao. May I

The empire seethed with discontent, the blame for which rests upon those who would interfere with the natural goodness of the heart of man.

ask what is the essence of this perfect Tao? I desire to obtain the essence of the universe to secure good harvests and feed my people. I should like also to control the yin and yang principles to fulfil the life of all living things."

"What you are asking about," replied Kuangch'engtse, "is merely the dregs of things. What you wish to control are the disintegrated factors thereof. Ever since the empire was governed by you, the clouds have rained before thickening, the foliage of trees has fallen before turning yellow, and the brightness of the sun and moon has increasingly paled. You have the shallowness of mind of a glib talker. How then are you fit to speak of perfect Tao?"

The Yellow Emperor withdrew. He resigned the Throne. He built himself a solitary hut, and sat upon white straw. For three months he remained in seclusion, and then went again to see Kuangch'engtse.

The latter was lying with his head towards the south. The Yellow Emperor approached from below upon his knees. Kowtowing twice upon the ground, he said, "I am told that you are in possession of perfect Tao. May I ask how to order one's life so that one may have long life?"

Kuangch'engtse jumped up with a start. "A good question indeed!" cried he. "Come, and I will speak to you of perfect Tao. The essence of perfect Tao is profoundly mysterious; its extent is lost in obscurity. "See nothing; hear nothing; guard your spirit in quietude and your body will go right of its own accord.

"Be quiet, be pure; toil not your body, perturb not your vital essence, and you will live for ever.

"For if the eye sees nothing, and the ear hears nothing, and the mind thinks nothing, your spirit will stay in your body, and the body will thereby live for ever.

"Cherish that which is within you, and shut off that which is without for much knowledge is a curse.

"Then I will take you to that abode of Great Light to reach the Plateau of Absolute Yang. I will lead you through the Door of the Dark Unknown to the Plateau of the Absolute Yin.

"The Heaven and Earth have their separate functions. The yin and yang have their hidden root. Guard carefully your body, and material things will prosper by themselves." ◻

Extract from the *Zhuangzi*, 3rd century BCE.

"I'm in two minds about dualism."

Documentaries

To view the documentaries below
and many others, visit
newphilosopher.com/videos/

Libbers

World in the balance – the people's paradox

www.newphilosopher.com/videos/libbers/

www.newphilosopher.com/videos/world-in-the-balance

Acclaimed filmmaker Vanessa Engle turns her attention to sexual politics in a three-part documentary series about feminism and its impact on women's lives today. Charting the rise of the women's liberation movement in the 1970s, this documentary series includes interviews with legendary British and American feminists, such as Kate Millett, Susan Brownmiller and Germaine Greer, and the last ever interview with novelist Marilyn French, who died in May 2009.

It took all of human history for the world's population to reach its first billion in 1800. Now we add a new billion nearly every dozen years. Over the next half century, 98 per cent of that growth will take place in our planet's poorest regions, and as the global total swells to nearly 9 billion by 2050, the social and environmental strains will be enormous. In Japan, Europe and Russia, birth rates are shrinking and the population is ageing, but in parts of India and Africa, more than half of the still growing population is under 25. The surprising conclusion is that the world population is now careening in two dramatically different directions.

Around the web

**New Philosopher is on
Twitter and Facebook, join us!**

How stone stacking wreaks havoc

In the past decade or so, there has been an explosion of cairns (stone stacks) around the world – in national parks, in the Scottish Highlands, on the beaches of Aruba. Park rangers, environmentalists, and hikers have all become alarmed, to varying degrees. The movement of so many stones can cause erosion, damage animal ecosystems, disrupt river flow, and confuse hikers, who depend on sanctioned cairns for navigation in places without clear trails.

newyorker.com/culture/rabbit-holes/

people-are-stacking-too-many-stones

The best books on Confucius

As Confucianism makes a comeback in China and its ideas become more, Daniel A. Bell, a professor of philosophy at Tsinghua University in Beijing, lists which books to read for an understanding of Confucius and his legacy.

fivebooks.com/best-books/confucius/

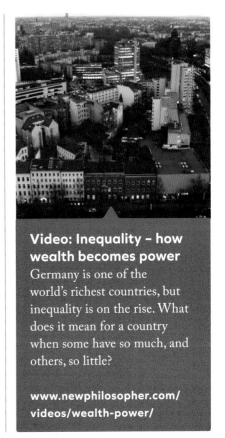

Video: Inequality – how wealth becomes power

Germany is one of the world's richest countries, but inequality is on the rise. What does it mean for a country when some have so much, and others, so little?

**www.newphilosopher.com/
videos/wealth-power/**

Devil's dictionary

AMBIDEXTROUS, ADJ. Able to pick with equal skill a right-hand pocket or a left.

@ethics_centre
"Virtue ethics is arguably the oldest ethical theory, originating in Ancient Greece. It defines the ethical life as one dedicated to developing ethical virtues of character. Good actions = virtuous character. Bad actions = vices."

Follow New Philosopher on social media

Biased news media or biased readers?

Gallup survey data indicates that Americans are increasingly distrustful about potentially biased news. They might also want to worry about the partiality of their own judgement as well as how their news consumption habits may affect it. The bias consumers bring with them distorts their rating of news content, new research shows, and those who are most distrustful of the news media tend to be the most biased readers.

nytimes.com/2018/09/26/upshot/biased-news-media-or-biased-readers-an-

experiment-on-trust.html

What's on

Sydney Writers' Festival
Sydney, Australia

April 29 - May 5, 2019

Sydney Writers' Festival presents more than 300 events, attracting audiences of 100,000 plus for a week-long conversation of books and ideas. The festival brings together some of the world's most curious and compassionate, irreverent but respectful, intelligent and argumentative writers. With the finest writing and storytelling at its core, their programming is driven by the ideas and issues that animate all types of literature. Previous international guests include Neil Gaiman, Susan Faludi, Paul Beatty, Colson Whitehead, Anne Enright, Armando Iannucci, Roxane Gay, Carol Ann Duffy, Ian Rankin, Gloria Steinem, Julian Barnes, Alice Walker, George Saunders, and many more.

www.swf.org.au/

Keith Haring Exhibition
Tate Liverpool. Liverpool, UK

June 14 - November 10, 2019

A part of the legendary New York art scene of 1980s, Haring was a champion of his generation's counterculture. Inspired by graffiti, pop art and underground club culture, Haring worked with like-minded artists such as Andy Warhol and Jean-Michel Basquiat, all of whom were deeply interested in creating art for the many, and used new media and public spaces, not galleries to do so. Compelled to speak for his generation, Haring's art responds to urgent issues including political dictatorship, racism, homophobia, drug addiction, AIDS awareness, capitalism, and the environment.

www.tate.org.uk/whats-on/tate-liverpool/exhibition/keith-haring

Here We Are
The Art Gallery of NSW
Sydney, Australia

August 24 – October 13, 2019

Taking its title from a 2016 painting by New Zealand artist Kushana Bush, this exhibition explores the intensity, intricacy, pathos and power of human relationships through remarkable new acquisitions for the Art Gallery of NSW collection by some of the most compelling women artists at work today – from Australia's Tracey Moffatt, Judith Wright, and Justene Williams to internationally renowned figures Jenny Saville, Dana Schutz, Tracey Emin, Njideka Akunyili Crosby, and Kimsooja.

www.artgallery.nsw.gov.au/exhibitions/here-we-are/

Whether you're a philosopher or a bookworm, there are plenty of events to pique your interest – from Chicago to Sydney.

Friedrich Nietzsche and the Artists of the New Weimar

National Gallery of Canada. Ottawa, Canada

April 18 – August 25, 2019

By the time he died in 1900, Friedrich Nietzsche had become one of the most influential thinkers of his time. Often seen as a radical prophet of modernism, he had a major impact on the artistic and cultural world of Weimar Germany in the late 19th and early 20th centuries. The exhibition features a famed bronze sculpture of the celebrated Philosopher by German artist Max Klinger as its centrepiece, as well as a variety of work from the likes of Henry van de Velde, Edvard Munch, Curt Stoeving and others, and explores the creation of an 'official Nietzsche' by Klinger and his patrons, and looks at how an iconic sculpture ultimately became a cult image.

www.gallery.ca/whats-on/exhibitions-and-galleries/masterpiece-in-focus-friedrich-nietzsche-and-the-artists-of-the

Christien Meindertsma: Everything Connects

The Art Institute of Chicago. Chicago, USA

March 21 – October 20, 2019

What can you do with an entire harvest of flax, or 1000 wool sweaters? The possibilities are endless and entwined. By exploring the often-hidden lives of products within their social, political, and material contexts, Meindertsma invites us to reconsider the value of objects, especially the potential of undervalued resources such as flax and recycled wool. Her projects suggest that intelligent processes and design can play an important role in addressing the overconsumption of resources and prompting positive change.

www.artic.edu/exhibitions/9224/christien-meindertsma-everything-connects

HowTheLightGetsIn

Hay-on-Wye, UK

24 – 27 May, 2019

HowTheLightGetsIn, the world's largest philosophy and music festival, is back in 2019. Headlining the 2019 festival are the likes of Saul Kripke, Liz Truss, and Terry Eagleton, who will be joined by philosophers, scientists, artists, musicians, comedians, and writers for debate, talks, music, and late-night parties. The festival prides itself on being about ideas and wonder, and creating a space where everyone's imagination can flourish – a place where you can discover ground-breaking ideas that have yet to make their mark.

www.howthelightgetsin.org/hay

Subscribe to
New Philosopher

3 ways
to subscribe

(1) Send your details along with the form on the next page to:
130 Macquarie St, Hobart TAS 7000 Australia

(2) Online at
https://www.newphilosopher.com/subscribe/

(3) Email us: **subscribe@newphilosopher.com**

The perfect gift for family & friends

Extraordinary quality in all respects. *New Philosopher* is one of the best things happening.

I love how the writing reminds me that the types of issues we are grappling with today are similar to those grappled with by philosophers for centuries.

I love this magazine. I no longer like reading or listening to mainstream news as it is not good for my health. Your magazine is good for me. It has real discussions that relate to life rather than reporting sensational 'news'. Thank you.

what our readers say

Your magazine is so helpful and is churning up the little grey cells, as Hercule Poirot says.

Thank you, this world is brighter, more aware, and more meaningful with your publication in it.

Great magazine. Finally one worth reading. Will recommend it to all friends.

This is a quality magazine: intelligent, lucid, lively, and beautifully designed and produced. Recommended.

A magazine that treats its audience as intellectual equals, that doesn't insult their intelligence by simplifying or manipulating concepts or appealing to crass consumerism as do most of the publications out there. Thank you for creating something that brings philosophy out of the sandstone universities and into our lounge rooms without losing its depth or critical stance.

You have introduced such a wonderfully fresh & intelligent publication to expand our minds & hearts. Thank you.

I feel like I have been waiting for this magazine all my life.

In a country so defined by the shallow, crass propaganda and cognitive conformity coming out of its papers, magazines, and broadcasters, yours is a true gem. You have no idea how happy I was to discover it, it has given me hope for the future of this country's media landscape and for the public discussion emanating from it.

I have to say that it is a tremendous relief and joy that your publication has arrived. Your magazine provides oxygen to the soul. I have often felt alone, alienated or old-fashioned in my outlook but now know I have a soulmate to reflect and take action with, namely *New Philosopher*.

SUBSCRIPTION

1-year subscription

☐ $60 AU/US, €39 UK, €55 EU/CAN, $55 NZ, €65 Rest of the world

2-year subscription

☐ $115 AU/US, €75 UK, €105 EU/CAN, $160 NZ, €125 Rest of the world

3-year subscription

☐ $150 AU/US, €110 UK, €140 EU/CAN, $220 NZ, €159 Rest of the world

Note: AU in AUD, US/NZ in USD, Rest of the world in EUR

I would like to start my subscription from:

☐ issue #24 'balance'   ☐ issue #25

I would like to purchase back issues at AUD$17.95

(AUD$25 NZ, USD$25 ROW, includes postage)

☐ #7 'health' ☐ #8 'travel' ☐ #9 'property' ☐ #10 'fame'

☐ #11 'technology' ☐ #12 'education' ☐ #13 'luck'

☐ #14 'nature' ☐ #15 'future' ☐ #16 'food'

☐ #17 'communication' ☐ #18 'stuff' ☐ #19 'life'

☐ #20 'play' ☐ #21 'power' ☐ #22 'time'

☐ #23 'being human'

Note: issues #1-6 are sold out; back issues shipped from the UK and Australia.

My details:

Name _____

Address _____

Suburb _____

State _____

Postcode _____

Country _____

Email _____

I am buying this subscription as a gift.
Please deliver to:

Name _____

Address _____

Suburb _____

State _____

Postcode _____

Country _____

Email _____

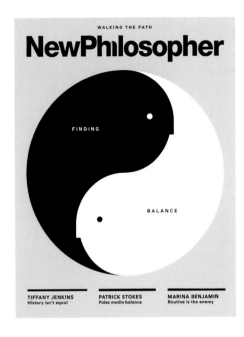

Credit card payment:

Charge my:

☐ Visa   ☐ Mastercard

Card No.: _____

Signature: _____ Expiry date __ /__

CVV: _____ Amount: $ _____

Note that you can also subscribe online at:
https://www.newphilosopher.com/subscribe/

Cheque payment (<u>Australia</u> only):

☐ I have enclosed an Australian cheque made payable to *New Philosopher*

Cheque no.: _____

Amount: $ _____

Please return to:

New Philosopher
130 Macquarie St, Hobart TAS 7000 Australia

Illustration by Aida Novoa & Carlos Egan

by **Nigel Warburton**

The golden mean of industriousness

It is a cliché of our times that work has wormed its way into the home, eating away at our free time. On this view we are, in Jean-Jacques Rousseau's words, "born free, but everywhere are in chains". With Wi-Fi and a smartphone, you are never really away from your office if something needs doing. Indeed, the office, a place where you go to work, is a thing of the past for many – it has become an abstract concept, a virtual set of relations, not a physical space. We just work where we happen to be, interacting with co-workers, clients, and the public in a complex web of relations. We receive emails and phone calls, do things, reply to people, click on buttons, stuff happens, and we get paid for this if all goes well. It has untethered many people from their desks, and has created the phenomenon of

the digital nomad, a peripatetic distance worker with a laptop who can just as easily work from a hotel lobby in an exotic country as in a coffee bar in the suburbs.

Some consequences of this are good; others bad. As a species we have evolved over millions of years to be social animals who interact well face-to-face in smallish groups. Even the realism of video conferencing is still a poor substitute for in-the-flesh interactions: the subtleties of interpersonal interaction are not all captured by a web camera. In the age of digital technology, embodied encounters still have a part to play.

But what is a good balance between work and the rest of our lives? Some gurus of productivity would have us toiling for long hours, others reducing our daily work burden to four hours or fewer. It's easy to say that for a successful life you need to get work into proportion, and not allow it to creep into your every waking moment, spoiling your relationships with friends and family, and gradually wearing you down until you seem to exist simply to deal with work issues. But what is proportion here?

For Aristotle, virtues always fall between two vices: bravery, for example, lies between the vices of foolhardiness (where you have no concern whatsoever for your safety), and cowardice (where you cannot bring yourself to do the right thing). What is the golden mean of industriousness? The two obvious contenders for it to lie between are laziness (when you can't be bothered to work at all), and workaholism (when you just can't stop working). The virtue of industriousness can be attractive. But merely working isn't a good in itself. As Karl Marx and his followers well knew, mere industriousness and working for someone else's gain risks turning you into a cog in a machine, alienated from the things you are making, from the process of its production, and from what you might actually make of your life. What we want, most of us at least, is meaningful work and meaningful leisure time. Those caught up in the worst excesses of capitalism have little chance of becoming fulfilled through spending more time away from work: the terms of work are dictated from above. Here I am not just talking of those in manual jobs: many working

Constant distraction from the task in hand is obviously not good in itself.

in the world of finance and law have to work excessively long hours too. Yet the gig economy, with its seeming freedoms and flexibility can be just as much of a grindstone. Low wages and fluctuating availability of work means that those who choose this way of living often push themselves very hard to earn a decent pay cheque. It is no good having the option to spend more time not working if the consequence is such a low level of income that this freedom cannot be enjoyed. The taxi driver who 'chooses' when to work is not really 'free' if he or she has to work ten hours or more a day to make enough to live on.

It's not just employers who more or less compel their employees to have their apps open and ready with notifications on, and to check emails throughout the evening. Many of us have, in a short time, become addicted to the smartphone to such an extent that we feel bereft if we misplace it. I certainly do. Some philosophers have seriously suggested that your smartphone is literally part of your extended mind – it is simply an external memory bank, and much more. (If you lose your phone, then, on this view, you lose a bit of your mind.)

Fiendish designers have come up with brightly-coloured icons and rewarding activities that keep us hunched over these machines for many more hours a day than we intend to, and then leave us unable to get a proper night's sleep. When we wake up, the day begins with a ritual email check. There seems little hope for a pure experience of home away from work for any but those with a will of iron.

It's easy to bewail this phenomenon as an invasion of family life. But there are other ways of thinking about this too. Constant distraction from the task in hand is obviously not good in

itself. Yet there are some consolations. One in particular appeals to me as a writer. Imagine that you are held under water for half a minute, then allowed to surface to breathe. That first breath will taste sweet, and you'll very likely enjoy the fresh air after thinking you might drown. Think of your state underwater as having -3 units of pleasure, and your above water state as reaching a peak of 4 units of positive pleasure – then, removing the foot from your head might make you feel as much as 7 units better off than when you were submerged. Similarly, after hours of interruption and distraction provided by the small screen in your pocket, think of the quality of this newfound freedom if you are able to turn this smartphone off for a few hours of focused work. Most people don't manage to do this. But an electronic timer safe will help: you can turn off your smartphone and place it inside the safe, turn the dial, and set the opening time for, say two hours' time. Now there is no way the smartphone can bother you. Add to this an app that blocks all or most of the sites you might be lured to on the internet, and you are in business. You breathe in the fresh air of two hours of concentrated writing time. Like Ulysses tying himself to the mast to avoid being lured on to the rocks by the Sirens, you will have blocked your tendency to check your phone again and again. It isn't just having the two hours clear that feels good, it is having two hours that are so much clearer than any two hours in a world of interruptions and distractions. It's the contrast that makes those two hours seem especially valuable. Try it. ◘

"We need to talk about your shirk/life balance."

"Those who make peaceful revolution impossible will make violent revolution inevitable."

John F. Kennedy

Photo: G20 protest, London, UK, by Charlotte Gilhooly

13 questions:

Nayef Al-Rodhan

**In conversation
with Zan Boag**

Professor Nayef Al-Rodhan is a philosopher, neuroscientist, and geostrategist.

What is your demon?
I don't have one.

What is the most important part of your education?
University.

Which "thinker" has had the greatest influence on your life?
Averroes (Ibn-Rushd).

What do you doubt most?
Altruism.

If you could change one thing about the world, what would that be?
No more fear.

What does 'balance' mean to you?
Happiness.

What illusion do you suffer from?
None.

What would you never do, no matter the price?
Never do harm.

If you could choose, what would you have for your last meal?
Nothing.

The question you'd most like to ask others?
What makes you tick?

Your favourite word?
Dignity.

What is a good death?
No such thing... but probably while asleep.

What is the meaning of life?
Whatever you make it to be. N

Illustration by Aida Novoa & Carlos Egan